UNIVERSITY OF NORTH CAROLINA
PUBLICATIONS OF THE DEPARTMENT OF ROMANCE LANGUAGES

General Editor: ALDO SCAGLIONE

Editorial Board: JUAN BAUTISTA AVALLE-ARCE, PABLO GIL CASADO, FRED M. CLARK, GEORGE BERNARD DANIEL, JANET W. DÍAZ, ALVA V. EBERSOLE, AUGUSTIN MAISSEN, EDWARD D. MONTGOMERY, FREDERICK W. VOGLER

NORTH CAROLINA STUDIES IN THE ROMANCE LANGUAGES AND LITERATURES

ESSAYS, TEXTS, TEXTUAL STUDIES, TRANSLATIONS, SYMPOSIA

Founder: URBAN TIGNER HOLMES

Editor: JUAN BAUTISTA AVALLE-ARCE
Associate Editor: FREDERICK W. VOGLER

Other publications of the Department: *Estudios de Hispanófila, Hispanófila, Romance Notes, Studia Raeto-Romanica*

Distributed by:

INTERNATIONAL SCHOLARLY BOOK SERVICE, INC.
P. O. BOX 4347
Portland, Oregon 97208
U. S. A.

NORTH CAROLINA STUDIES IN THE
ROMANCE LANGUAGES AND LITERATURES
Number 133

FRANCISCO DE OSUNA
AND
THE SPIRIT OF THE LETTER

FRANCISCO DE OSUNA
AND
THE SPIRIT OF THE LETTER

BY

LAURA CALVERT

CHAPEL HILL
NORTH CAROLINA STUDIES IN THE ROMANCE
LANGUAGES AND LITERATURES
U.N.C. DEPARTMENT OF ROMANCE LANGUAGES
1973

ISBN: 978-0-8078-9133-9

DEPÓSITO LEGAL: V. 3.566 - 1973

ARTES GRÁFICAS SOLER, S. A. - JÁVEA, 28 - VALENCIA (8) - 1973

CONTENTS

			Page
Preface ...			9
Chapter	I.	OSUNA AND HIS COMMENTATORS ...	11
		Osuna's Life and Work: Problems ...	11
		Structure and Style in the Castilian Works ...	22
—	II.	THE NATURAL LAW OF LOVE ...	31
		Love: the Unifying Force ...	36
		God, Man, and Angels ...	38
		Self-love ...	44
		The Will ...	47
		Natural Love and Grace ...	51
		Corazón y ánima ...	54
—	III.	MEDITATION AND CONTEMPLATION: CONCRETE AND ABSTRACT ...	57
		The Eagle ...	60
		Itinerary of Meditation ...	63
—	IV.	THE EAGLE DESCENDS: INCARNATION OF THE WORD ...	70
		The Expansion of Language ...	76
—	V.	OSUNA'S DIALECTIC AND RHETORIC ...	80
		Scripture and the Book of Creatures ...	80
		A Scriptural Exegesis ...	88
		Emotions ...	94
		Prolixity and Abbreviation ...	96
		Obscurity ...	98
—	VI.	MEDITATION OF A FIGURED PASSAGE ...	101
		The First Three Alphabets ...	101
		The Position of Treatise IV, Third Alphabet ...	103
		A Summary of Treatise IV ...	106
		The Heart and the Blood ...	112
		The Soul and the Body: Further Details on the Heart ...	113
		Some Theories about the Heart and the Blood ...	116

			Page
Chapter	VII.	SOME MAJOR FIGURES OF TREATISE IV ...	120
		Mutability of the Heart	120
		Figures of Will and Decision	125
		The Double Meaning of the Praeteritio	127
		The Castle, the Terrestrial Paradise and the Ark of the Covenant	129
—	VIII.	AN ANAGOGICAL LEVEL: ITS REVELATION AND ITS PURPOSE	137
		Symbols of the Virgin	137
		Some Cosmic Concepts Suggested by the Figures ...	142
		Time and Eternity: Universal and Particular	143
		Baptism	145
		Figurative Language	149
—	IX.	THE ALPHABETS: STYLE AND CONTENT ...	153
		The Plain Style	153
		The Figured Style	156
		Figures as a Memory Aid	157
		The Science and Art of Contemplation	158
		Osuna's Ideas and Style in Historical Perspective ...	161
		The Poetic of Correspondences	164
Index			169
Addenda			174

PREFACE

The following study has been some years in the making, and as was the case in the Alphabets of Osuna, a later work is to appear before an earlier one. These nine chapters were intended to show how Osuna uses mystical symbolism and allegory in his own writing and in the methods of meditation and contemplation he teaches. Unlike many other mystics, Osuna explains the philosophical and psychological bases of his methods. Before writing this text, I compiled an "encyclopaedia" of Osuna's symbols; this has not yet appeared in print. It seemed to me, however, that a study of Osuna's rationale and techniques of using symbol and allegory would be useful to others, whether interested specifically in the mystics or in the development of Baroque styles.

I am grateful to those who have helped me in this work, especially to Bruce Wardropper, who advised me at the beginning of the project, and to Kenneth Scholberg, who helped me finish it. For their assistance with the problem of bibliography I should like to thank especially those two, Luigi Borelli, the late Alexander Schutz, and Father Hofer and Father Leo Miller of the Josephinum. It is truly impossible for me to list here all the teachers, friends, colleagues, librarians and relatives who have helped me to obtain texts and to solve the many problems that presented themselves during the course of this study. I am indebted to the Graduate School at the Ohio State University for procuring a reproduction of *El norte de los estados*, and to the Humanities Division and the Library at the University of Maryland, Baltimore County, for having printed my microfilms of five of Osuna's works. Finally, I am most grateful to my editor at the University of North Carolina, Juan Bautista Avalle-Arce, for his excellent suggestions on this material.

In citing the texts under consideration, I have taken the liberty of modernizing the orthography when its archaisms presented an obstacle to easy reading. When books are numbered by folio, I have so indicated. Otherwise, unaccompanied Arabic numerals refer to pages. Within quotations, annotations to Biblical chapter and verse are in parentheses if supplied by the source. Those supplied by me are in brackets. All the texts of Osuna's works that I used are listed in the notes to Chapter I. In these notes the titles of Osuna's Latin works are also to be found.

Osuna's comments on any one topic often are scattered through many works. Because of this it has been necessary to include many locus cites. I have reduced all the works to short titles after the first complete bibliographical entry, so as to distract the reader as little as possible. Numbered footnotes contain bibliographical information or additional comments related to the text.

In the course of this study I have posed some questions to which I have not supplied answers. Some of these questions fall into the fields of history, history of ideas, theology, or iconography, as well as literature. I hope that this study may call to the attention of others the largely neglected body of interesting material that is to be found in the works of Osuna. For this reason, I have invited the reader to speculate with me, at several points, about matters yet to be fully explored.

Chapter One of the following text is an attempt to place Osuna in the context of his historical moment. In the succeeding chapters I have tried to supply enough information about Osuna's philosophy, rhetoric, materials and methods to explicate one of Osuna's texts, and to facilitate the reader's understanding of other Osunian works. In the last chapter, I have drawn some tentative conclusions about Osuna's place in the development of baroque literary styles.

For the sake of Osuna and of my family and friends, I wish that this manuscript might be the model of perfection that they all deserve. As it is, I acknowledge sole responsibility for its errors and eccentricities.

Laura Calvert

Chapter I

OSUNA AND HIS COMMENTATORS

Osuna's life and work: problems. Francisco de Osuna (1492?-1541?) was the author of eight Castilian and six Latin books, on mental prayer and other aspects of Christian life, which were widely distributed in Spain and other countries during the sixteenth and seventeenth centuries. They appeared in a total of 59 editions in Spain, France, Belgium, and Italy, as well as in a number of translations into Italian, German, and Latin. An apocryphal German work, *Dess Teufels' Gaissl,* was attributed to him (Munich 1602). In spite of this evident popularity and the important role he played in Spanish mystical thought, we know only a few facts about his life, and only certain aspects of his work have been studied. One reason for this neglect is the inaccessibility of his books. Only two of them have appeared in modern editions. Another obstacle is the complex style that he uses, purposefully, in parts of all his Castilian works. This style relies heavily on the rhetorical methods of preachers and on a symbolism not generally understood in this century. I shall try to elucidate this in the following chapters.

Fortunately, Osuna also writes at times in a clear and simple style, in which he explains the ideas that govern his own techniques. At other times he uses the plain style to deliver criticisms of monarchy (he prefers democracy), or to defend converts and even heretics, although he is a Franciscan priest and, probably, a church official, writing at the time of the Inquisition. His interest in natural science leads him to discuss matters of interest to historians of physiology. Through one of his books (the Third

Alphabet)[1] he taught Sta. Teresa of Avila the procedures of mental prayer that she practiced for years, as she attests in her *Vida* (chap. IV). His works reveal to us many interesting aspects of life and letters during a critical period of Spanish history. Nevertheless, we still do not even know Osuna's family name, and only a few scholars have read more than one or two of his works.[2]

---

[1] Its full title is *Tercera parte del libro llamado Abecedario Spiritual agora nuevamente impreso é corregido y añadido* [sic] *la tabla de los tratados y capítulos que contiene. Escritores Místicos Españoles*, I; Nueva Biblioteca de Autores Españoles, XVI (Madrid, Bailly-Baillière, 1911). This is based on the 1544 edition published at Burgos. Unfortunately, the modern transcription is somewhat faulty. The book will be referred to hereafter as *3 Abc.*; similar short titles will be given to the other Alphabet Books.

From this NBAE edition an English translation has been made, *The Third Spiritual Alphabet*, translated from the Spanish by a Benedictine of Stanbrook (London: Burns Oates, 1931, and Westminster, Maryland: Newman Bookshop, 1948). From it also derives the Italian translation by Giovanni Bertini, *Frate Francisco de Osuna, Via alla mistica, terza parte dell'abecedario spirituale* (Brescia, Morcelliana, 1933). For a detailed bibliographical study, see the work of Father Fidèle de Ros listed in note 4.

The Fourth Alphabet (full title: *Ley de amor y quarta parte del Abecedario espiritual dõde se tratã muy de rayz los misterios y preguntas; y exercicios del amor: y la theologia que pertenece no menos al entendimiĕto q̃ a la voluntad: harto vtil avn para los predicadores q̃ dessean ver en buen romãce las cosas q̃ de si son escabrosas*) has appeared in *Místicos franciscanos españoles*, I, Biblioteca de Autores Cristianos (Madrid: Ed. Católica, 1948), and is the only other book by Osuna to appear in this century.

References in this work to the Third and Fourth Alphabets are to these editions. For the other works, the editions I have used are listed in note 2.

[2] The editions that I have used are as follows:

Primera parte del libro llamado Abecedario espiritual: q̃ trata de las circunstãcias de la sagrada passion del hijo de dios. compuesto por el padre fray Frãcisco de Ossuna (Zaragoza, Pedro Bernuz y Bartolome de Nagera, 1546). Location: University of Chicago Library.

Segunda parte del libro llamado Abecedario spiritual: donde se tratan diuersos exercicios en cada letra el suyo. Compuesto por el padre fray Frãcisco de Ossuna frayle menor (Burgos, Juan de Junta, 1555). Location: University of Chicago Library.

Quinta parte: del Abecedario spiritual de nueuo compuesta por el padre fray Francisco de Ossuna: q̃ es Consuelo de pobres y Auiso de ricos. No menos vtil para los frayles q̃ para los seculares y avn pa los predicadores. Cuyo intento deue ser retraer los hombres del amor de las riquezas falsas y hazerlos pobres de espiritu (Burgos, Juan de Junta, 1554). Location: Harvard University Library.

Sexta parte del Abecedario espiritual: Cõpuesto por el padre Fray Frãcisco de Ossuna: q̃ trata sobre las llagas de Jesu Christo. para exercicio de todas las personas deuotas. Añadidas las tablas de las otras cinco partes,

In recognition of this, Allison Peers remarked that Osuna is an enigma yet to be resolved.[3]

A solid foundation for further studies of Osuna was laid when Father Fidèle de Ros published in 1936 a full-length study of Osuna's religious doctrine, together with his bibliography and all available data on his life.[4] Father de Ros remarks in his preface that he had access to the information collected by Father Michel-Ange Sarraute, an earlier researcher in Franciscan history. Father Sarraute's articles[5] are useful in establishing Osuna's place in the history of religious movements in sixteenth century Spain. Father de Ros says also that Rodríguez Marín, *tocayo* of Osuna and a native of the same place, planned to publish a biography of Osuna to accompany a new edition of *El norte de los estados*, Osuna's book for laymen. But "ce même Rodríguez Marín confiait au P. Michel-Ange qu'il était quasi-impossible de mettre la main sur les documents concernant le maître de sainte Thérèse" [Osuna] (de Ros, *Maître*, XIV, n. 1).

Most of the available information about Osuna's life is drawn from his own works. Some comes from records or correspondence in the Franciscan order, and some from the inquisitorial process involving Francisco Ortiz, one of Osuna's friends, and Francesca

---

con la del Cōbite del sacramento: *que el mismo autor compuso. Nunca antes impressa* (Medina del Campo, Matheo y Francisco del Canto, 1554). Location: Harvard University Library.

Gracioso Cōbite de las gracias del sancto sacramēto del altar: hecho a todas las animas d'los cristianos principalmēte los religiosos: clerigos: mōjas: beatas: y deuotos d'la sacra comuniō y de la missa (Burgos, Juan de Junta, 1537). Location: British Museum.

Norte de los estados: En que se da regla de biuir a los Mācebos: y a los Casados: e a los Biudos: y a todos los cōntinētes. Y se tratā muy por estēso los remedios d'l desastrado casamiēto enseñando q̃ tal a de ser la vida del Cristiano casado. Cōpuesto por el reverēdo padre fray frācisco de Ossuna: commissario general de la ordē de sant frācisco. En las prouincias de las indias del mar occeano (Burgos, Juan de Junta, 1541). Location: Hispanic Society.

[3] E. Allison Peers, *The Spanish Mystics* (2nd ed., London and New York, 1951), I, 65.

[4] Fidèle de Ros, *Un maître de Sainte Thérèse, le père François d'Osuna, sa vie, son oeuvre, sa doctrine spiritual* (Paris, 1936).

[5] Michel-Ange Sarraute, "La vie franciscaine en Espagne entre les deux couronnements de Charles-quint," *Revista de Archivos, Bibliotecas y Museos*, XXIX, XXXI, and XXXII, 1913-14.

Hernández, the *alumbrada*. It has been impossible, as yet, to determine the exact dates of Osuna's birth and death. He himself says, in one of his Latin works, that as a boy (*puer*) he was present at the conquest of Tripoli by Navarro in 1510 (de Ros, *Maître*, 6). He also acknowledges the dependence of his family and himself on the house of the counts of Ureña, later to become the dukes of Osuna.

By 1523, Osuna was a member of the Friars Minor of the Regular (reformed) Observance, a preacher, and a consultant on questions of mental prayer (de Ros, *Maître*, 44-45). In 1527 he published the *Tercera parte del libro llamado Abecedario spiritual*, more generally known nowadays as the Third Alphabet. It is one of the first original spiritual treatises in Spain.[6] The *Primera parte* did not appear until 1528, although it is called by Osuna his "first fruits."[7] It contains a prologue to the first three "alphabetos o abecedarios." As the reader of these books will discover, this series of three books serves as an introduction to the theory and practice of meditation and contemplation. The books are graded as the titles indicate. The First Alphabet is elementary, and the next two carry the reader into ever more advanced phases of the subject. The books were published out of sequence, so that the public saw the more advanced materials first. No doubt this led to problems. A similar difficulty exists to this day. The Third and Fourth Alphabets are readily available to us, but the preparatory materials in Alphabets One and Two are not. Some of the enigmas seen in Osuna's work are solved simply by reading the books in their proper sequence.

In the prologue to the First Alphabet, the author clearly indicates that he had composed Alphabets One, Two and Three, at least in their basic form (a series of distichs in alphabetical order), at the time he wrote the prologue. These Alphabets are

---

[6] This is attested by Pierre Groult, *Les mystiques des Pays Bas et la littérature espagnole du 16ième siècle* (Louvain, 1927), 82.

[7] This statement appears on folio 3 in the first of two prologues to the First Alphabet. This prologue consists of a brief introduction and dedication to Juan Téllez Girón, count of Ureña. The next prologue introduces the first three Alphabets, and is entitled "prólogo primero" although it follows the other one. Perhaps it was written earlier, or was bound second by mistake.

divided into *tratados*, each of which is a gloss on one distich. Osuna says that he composed the brief sentences for his own edification and arranged them alphabetically as a memory aid. The resulting short alphabets were transmitted by his friends to others, who took the liberty of glossing the distichs in ways displeasing to Osuna. He therefore undertook to explicate the sentences according to his own intent (*1 Abc.*, fols. 4-5).

These three *Abecedarios*, then, existed in outline before any one of them was glossed or published. In the prologue to the Third Alphabet, Osuna says he has "medianamente concluido las dos [primeras] partes" (*3 Abc.*, 320); in the Second Alphabet (fol. 112), he refers to the relation among the letters P in Alphabets One, Two and Three. Evidently Osuna had all three books in mind as he worked on each one. This is shown by their own internal consistency as well as by the author's comments. For reasons that we can only speculate on, the Third Alphabet was published first.

The Second and Fourth Alphabets appeared in 1530. The series was completed by two books that appeared posthumously, the Fifth in 1542 and the Sixth in 1554. The titles of all these works designate them as parts of one spiritual alphabet book, although not all have internal alphabetical structure. [8]

In 1530 Osuna published the *Gracioso Combite de las gracias del Sancto Sacramento del altar*, a treatise on the Eucharist, and in 1531 *El norte de los estados*, a book on courtship, marriage, and family life. On the frontispiece of the latter work Osuna is called "comisario general de la orden de San Francisco en las provincias de las Indias del mar océano." It is conjectured that he held this post in 1528-29, although he never came to the New World (de Ros, *Maître*, 113-14). Both Father de Ros and Father

---

[8] The alphabetized distichs that form the most explicitly alphabetical aspect of Osuna's work are so composed that they could have been written either before or after the corresponding chapters or treatises themselves. They occur briefly in the Fourth Alphabet, but there they do not govern the internal subdivisions of the work; it is clear that the author did not intend them to. In all the other Alphabets, however, treatises or chapters are headed by such distichs, except in the last part of the Fifth. Here, Osuna may have abandoned the device, or, possibly, he may have died before completing that portion of the work.

Sarraute point out the curious fact that the annalist Wadding names the Franciscan visitor-general to the Indies, a subordinate post, but does not tell who held the superior position, that of "comisario general." This strange omission is one of many aspects of Osuna's life still unexplained.

In 1532 Osuna arrived in France. He published two collections of Latin sermons in 1533: *Sanctuarium Biblicum* (Toulouse), and *Pars Meridionalis* (Paris). He spent the years 1534 to 1536 in Antwerp, where four other Latin books were printed (de Ros, *Maître*, 139-46).[9]

The Fifth Alphabet, written after Osuna's return to Spain, carries a dedication to Antonio de Guevara. This dedication, however, was written by the bookseller Juan de Espinosa, not by Osuna, so it does not necessarily establish a personal relationship between Osuna and Guevara. In these pages, the bookseller says that Osuna is dead; he does not give a precise date. The first edition of the book is dated 1542 (de Ros, *Maître*, 168).

The Sixth Alphabet was not published until 1554, but its dedication had been written by the author himself. This Alphabet

---

[9] Titles of the Latin works are as follows:
Sanctuarium biblicum solertissimi Patris fratris Francisci de Ossuna ... in cujus fine tanquam in loco archae foederis reperies deiparae Virginis sermones octo, sub hoc themate: "Ipsa conteret caput tuum" pro sabbatis Quadragesimae ac Resurrectione sequenti. (Also known as *Sermones de Sanctis* or *Pars Septentrionalis*.)
Pars meridionalis, in accommodas hisce temporibus allegorias: hermeniasque mirabiles Evangeliorum Dominicalium totius anni a Bibliographo patre Fratre Francisco ab Ossuna, Bethico ...
Expositionis super "Missus est" alter (sic: for *primus*) *Liber, ubi agitur de hominis reformatione in paradiso deliciarum deformati, ac per Incarnationem filii Dei in paradiso Virginea reparati ...*
Alter Sermonum liber super "Missus est," ubi per omnes missiones sacrae paginae, causae accommodas, agitur de ipso adventu filii Dei vario, exordiens a festo beati Andreae per singulas ferias, dñicas et festa usque ad epiphaniam inclusive ... (The last is also known as *Pars Orientalis*.) Both these expositions of "Missus est" appeared in one volume.
Pars Occidentalis, in accommodas hisce temporibus Evangeliorum quadragesimalium expositiones, a dominica Septuagesimae usque ad feriam secundam Resurrectionis. Ad haec septem sermones beatae Mariae sub hoc "Beatus venter qui te portavit" pro diebus sabbatinis; et Passio compassionis Christi ...
Trilogium evangelicum. Primum Christi passionem ... docet ..., Proximum vero Resurrectionem ... Tertium autem Christi ascensionem ...
For the above, I am indebted to Father de Ros (*Maître*, 169-71). I have been unable to obtain the Latin works.

is a return to elementary phases of meditation, like those of the First. The Sixth is a treatise on the wounds of Christ; the First is a treatise on the Passion. In both, Osuna emphasizes the necessity of repeating these more humble — that is, less abstract — exercises. Perhaps this indicates that Osuna viewed the Sixth as the conclusion of his series of Alphabets, since in it he has come full circle, back to the concrete historical figure of Christ. The circle is the dominant motif of the Fourth Alphabet, and with its symbolic significance, it might have seemed an appropriate overall design for the Alphabet series. If the Sixth was the end of the series, as its title suggests, we are again confronted with an instance in which a later member of the series was completed before an earlier one. It is the Fifth that was left without Osuna's dedication, and it carried the news of his death. Also, its alphabetical apparatus was unfinished. We have already seen that Osuna apparently worked from a primary scheme that enabled him to write Alphabets One, Two and Three concurrently. He may have distributed sermons and materials for meditation or for pedagogy among several ongoing projects. Such a technique of composition would explain certain features of the internal structure of his works, in which figures like the eagle or the dove appear "dismembered" and scattered through various books, while still showing a consistent symbolic value on allegorical, tropological or anagogical levels. In the case of the Fifth Alphabet, unlike the first three, composition of the text apparently preceded that of the alphabetical distich.

Osuna's titles show that he conceived of the six Alphabet Books as parts of one enormous work. He organizes the books into segments based on a text, a figure or a concept. Many of these segments may originally have been sermons. These could be created in accordance with the larger scheme, and each one assigned to its appropriate "part" as the weeks went by. Since the Sixth Alphabet was planned as a shorter work than the Fifth, it would naturally be finished before the Fifth if both were begun at the same time. The Sixth may also have been hastened because it was demanded by the Duchess of Béjar, as reported by Osuna in his prologue (fol. 2).

In spite of the late publication date of the Sixth Alphabet, I see no reason to doubt that it is an authentic work of Osuna. He could well have finished the Sixth before his death, only to have its publication delayed by the enormous project of the indexes that accompany it. These cover the entire series of Alphabets and the *Convite*. The indexes show the work of more than one hand; the basis for selection of index items changes noticeably. I suspect that Osuna himself began them but could not finish them.

Father Sarraute at one time considered the Sixth Alphabet to be apocryphal,[10] but Father de Ros apparently does not. He has weeded out various other attributions he considered to be false.

The indexes that accompany the Sixth Alphabet are by scriptural text (in Latin) and by topic (in Spanish). Such a method suggests that the books were used as source materials for other preachers. This conjecture is confirmed by the testimony of Mathias Weynsen, one of Osuna's superiors, to this effect (de Ros, *Maître*, 608). Osuna's words and ideas, apparently, were disseminated orally as well as in the numerous editions of his works. It is no wonder that his traces appear in the works of his contemporaries and successors, though often without proper credit.

Osuna's books suffered few deletions by the inquisitorial censor until the suppression of the *Convite* in 1559. Sainz Rodríguez attributes this suppression to the fact that Osuna favored frequent communion, a topic that had become sensitive because it was also advocated by the *alumbrados*.[11] Osuna's position in relation to this sect — if it was a sect — has been the subject of some disagreement. Boehmer, in his history of the judicial process against Francisco Ortiz and Francesca Hernández, called Osuna an "Änhanger" of the *alumbrada*, Francesca. There was, in fact, testimony to Osuna's admiration of her, and his friendship for her defender, Francisco Ortiz.[12] The proceedings against this

---

[10] Gaston Etchegoyen, *L'Amour divin: Essai sur les sources de Sainte Thérèse* (Paris, 1923), 39-41.

[11] Pedro Sainz Rodríguez, *Espiritualidad española* (Madrid, 1961), 212.

[12] Eduard Boehmer, *Franzisca Hernandez und Frai Franzisco Ortiz, Anfänge Reformatorischer Bewegungen in Spanien unter Kaiser Karl V* (Leipzig, 1865), 26.

friend may be one of the reasons for Osuna's bitter criticism of the ecclesiastical hierarchy in the Fifth Alphabet.

The matter of doctrinal differences is a complicated one. Marcel Bataillon has discussed the fairly close relationship between Franciscan spirituality and illuminism. He also compares Osuna's doctrine of *recogimiento* with the *dejamiento* of the *alumbrados*.[13] The task of comparison is complicated by the fact that the doctrine of *dejamiento* never found a spokesman as systematic or eloquent as Osuna. It apears that one difference between the *alumbrados* and Franciscan mystics like Osuna was in their attitudes toward external evidence of ecstasy. The *alumbrados* expressed suspicion and downright disapproval of such manifestations (Bataillon, *Erasmo*, 170-71). Osuna cautions practitioners of contemplation to try to suppress ecstatic symptoms, for fear of criticism, but he does not see anything innately wrong with them. Another difference noted by Bataillon is the relatively greater emphasis placed by the *alumbrados* on mortification of the flesh. Paradoxically, this was accompanied by a few instances of license among practitioners of illuminism. According to the Edict issued against them, their doctrine of abandonment to the will of God led to the conclusion that the individual who was "illuminated" could no longer sin. Statements cited by Bataillon from *alumbrados*, however, cast doubt on the truth of this allegation (Bataillon, *Erasmo*, 172-73). If the *alumbrados* did really believe in impeccability they disagreed sharply with Osuna.

Osuna agrees with the *alumbrados* that sincere subjective prayer is of greater merit than mere participation in ritual. Osuna's doctrine of the sacraments seems, however, to accord them an importance greater than that seen by the *alumbrados*. Nevertheless, his idea of a purely spiritual baptism and communion could lie at the root of the notion expressed by Francisco Ortiz that "Christ is found more perfectly present in the souls of the just than in communion" (Bataillon, *Erasmo*, 171). This could mean simply that the corporal act of taking the bread and wine is secondary to the mental concept of its significance. If it does mean this, Osuna could subscribe to the statement too. Moreover,

---

[13] Marcel Bataillon, *Erasmo y España*, transl. Antonio Alatorre, (second Spanish ed., Mexico, 1966).

Osuna uses the term *alumbrar* in its multiple senses (see chap. IV and n. 1) to express concepts fundamental to his doctrine. This suggests a relationship between Osuna and the reformers known by the term *alumbrados*.

Osuna has left a voluminous and scholarly study of spiritual exercises, and his ideas are fairly well defined. Those of others often are not, as Bataillon has said (*Erasmo*, 174) and Father de Ros too (*Maître*, 77-105). For example, much of what we know of the *alumbrados* comes from the reports of their enemies. Angela Selke de Sánchez concludes that Franciscan spirituality was the basis of both *recogimiento* and *dejamiento*.[14] Bataillon notes that Franciscan mysticism probably prepared the ground for other spiritual movements.

Osuna's interest in Hebrew and in non-christian Latin and Greek sources, together with his defense of *conversos*, leads one inevitably to wonder if he himself was a convert. This could account for the scarcity of data on his family history, and the fact that his name does not appear as *comisario general* of the Indies. In his discussion of spiritual exercises, Osuna says that even infidels can achieve the grace of contemplation. (This grace is the actual unitive experience.) Because infidels can share this grace, some people say that Christians should not seek it, Osuna says (*3 Abc.*, 370). He, however, believes that non-Christians of the past not only practiced spiritual exercises but saved their souls thereby (*3 Abc.*, 483; *5 Abc.*, fols. 186-87).

Bataillon says that converts from Judaism were especially active in the spiritual ferment of this period (*Erasmo*, 181). Osuna's philosophy holds a special consolation for the *converso*, whether he himself was one or not.

Osuna's works cover many different forms of spiritual exercises. Most of these he synopsized in the Second Alphabet. In addition, his doctrine is systematic and complete, and supported by citations from Scripture and from philosophers and theologians. His works supply a context, therefore, to the ideas of

---

[14] However, Angela Selke de Sánchez has distinguished certain ideas that she believes typical of the *alumbrados* in "Vida y muerte de Juan López de Celain, alumbrado vizcaíno," *Bulletin Hispanique*, LXII, 2 (1960), 136-62.

the day, including those of Erasmianism as well as illuminism and Franciscan mysticism. The problem of his difficult style, combined with the inaccessibility of his books, has prevented our utilizing his information to the full.

Osuna's scholarly citations also demonstrate a further problem in determining the reciprocal influences among spiritual movements: that of common sources. Christian literature in all its variety supplied already the elements that each movement chose to emphasize (see Bataillon, *Erasmo*, 185). For this reason it is difficult to trace with certainty direct influences of Erasmus on Osuna, although there are points of resemblance. One is noted by Bataillon (*Erasmo*, 187). A particularly important parallel that the reader will remark is the emphasis by both on the spirit, rather than the letter, of the sacred books (see Bataillon, *Erasmo*, 198-99 for Erasmus' statement). The idea, however, is at least as old as St. Paul: "for the letter killeth, but the spirit giveth life" (II Cor. 3:6).

Although Osuna is critical of the hierarchy, his doctrine, by all accounts, is orthodox. A few minor errors are pointed out by de Ros. The contemporary censors found little to delete. Osuna did not publish at all until two years after the Edict against the *alumbrados*. This gave him a chance, as Bataillon has said (*Erasmo*, 174), to avoid risky statements. Perhaps this accounts for the delay in publishing Alphabets One and Two, and Osuna's comment that his distichs has been glossed by others in ways he did not like. They may have been glossed in ways prohibited by the Edict. If this were the case, we probably owe to this circumstance the precise explanations and bounteous scholarly apparatus of Osuna's works. He left little room for misinterpretation, and supported his statements by citing reputable sources.

On the question of mental prayer as taught by Osuna, opinions have varied depending on what text or texts the scholar reporting has read. Bataillon, who cites the Third Alphabet principally, does not discuss Osuna's other spiritual exercises, such as the meditation of the Passion, which Osuna advises as a prelude to *recogimiento*. This meditation is an important topic in the First Alphabet. Bataillon is correct when he notes that Osuna says that the idea of any concrete entity, even the human Christ, is an obstacle to mystical union. For this reason, according to Osuna, one should proceed to *recogimiento* — "no pensar nada." Bataillon recognizes Osuna's unusual merits as an explicator of *recogimiento*. On the other hand, Pfandl says that Osuna goes no further in his doctrine than a state of preparation for mysticism: that is, only as far as "no pensar nada." According to Pfandl, Osuna is simply a practitioner of mental prayer, not a theorist.[15] Pierre Groult reports that Osuna limited himself to easy and practical suggestions for attaining the grace of mystical prayer, leaving his reader only at the threshold of the mystical experience (Groult, *Mystiques*, 108-09 and fn. 1). However, Father de Ros, who unlike Groult and Pfandl has studied all the Castilian and Latin works, asserts that Osuna does not detain his disciple at the threshold of the mystic life, but rather seems to depict, at times, the closest possible union with God (de Ros, *Maître*, 533). To resolve the question of what Osuna actually does say about the unitive experience requires a close study of the works, with their complex figured style. When the system of Osuna's symbolism is understood, questions of content are the more readily resolved. His symbolism is closely associated with the spiritual exercise he calls the meditation of the creatures.

Whether Osuna is a simple practioner, as Pfandl says, or a learned and profound theorist as Father Sarraute (*Vie*, XXXI, 162) and Father Nazario de Santa Teresa [16] would have him, is a matter perhaps peripheral to this study. Nevertheless, some inferences may be drawn in the course of the following chapters.

Structure and style in the Castilian works. This study was begun for the purpose of investigating some of the structural and stylistic problems that have contributed to the lack of agreement about Osuna's work. No literary study of him has previously appeared, although Peers pointed out the need for such investigation. Father de Ros included a complete chapter (*Maître*, 394-423), as well as scattered comments, on style. He speaks of Osuna's methods of amplification, especially of his allegorical interpretation

---

[15] Ludwig Pfandl, *Historia de la literatura nacional española en la edad de oro,* Transl. Jorge Rubió Balaguer (Barcelona, 1952), 175.

[16] Nazario de Santa Teresa, *Filosofía de la mística: análisis del pensamiento español* (Madrid-Buenos Aires, 1953), 459.

of the Bible and his analogies. These terms show that he identifies Osuna's procedures with the rhetorical method of amplification or development practiced by preachers. The comparison is appropriate, and its implications are significant: first, the materials for amplification may consist of information on any concrete or abstract entity or event imaginable; second, the techniques of amplification are based on those of Biblical exegesis. Osuna is a Biblical exegete who draws upon the allegorical and philological traditions. He uses the four time-honored levels of Biblical interpretation (literal, metaphorical, tropological, anagogical) in ways that will be seen in succeeding chapters of this essay. However, he interprets on several levels not only Biblical passages but also the conduct of man and the things of nature. In doing so, he draws the analogies of which Father de Ros speaks; frequently these are analogies between the activities of concrete and abstract entities. Therefore, any material entity may bear a number of abstract connotations, based on the attributes that Osuna assigns to the thing. Osuna's sources for such attributions and connotations are varied. He cites many references, including concordances, patristic works, St. Bernard, St. Bonaventure, the Victorines, Aristotle, Pliny, Seneca, Boethius, and others in great number. The multiplicity of Osuna's information sources makes it difficult to predict what attributes he may assign a given entity. For example, since he believes that the soul has two sets of functions, he represents it by a man with two heads. Osuna's own work is the surest source of data about the signification of any entity or event that he includes. In order to guide the reader's meditations on the "creatures" and their activities, Osuna included in the First Alphabet a great deal of information about them. In the Second, he described various spiritual exercises, including that of meditating on the creatures, which requires use of the data in the First. Further information about the creatures, and passages requiring knowledge of them, occur throughout the other works. The first two Alphabets greatly facilitate the comprehension of other works, and it is unfortunate that they are not as readily available as the Third and Fourth, in which the writer assumes that his reader has already learned considerable material. Osuna himself speaks of the importance of proceeding in an orderly way from the elementary beginnings through the middle to the end (*1 Abc.*, fols. 4,5); he speaks of this specifically in respect to his first three Alphabets. He also emphasizes the importance of a retentive memory, and of memorizing the material read.

The First Alphabet, besides serving as an introduction to the spiritual life, contains a long meditation of the Passion. Osuna advised this meditation as a preface to the exercise of *recogimiento*. The Passion is treated by Osuna not only on the human level, but also on the anagogical one: he applies to the Man what is said of the Word. This meditation may also take a reverse trend: Osuna divides the grandeur of Christ among diverse things as, he says, is done in the Scriptures, where Christ is called "eagle," "tree," etc. (*1 Abc.*, fol. 104). Tracing the grandeur of the Word in such beings is the exercise Osuna calls contemplation of the creatures. San Juan de la Cruz also refers to this exercise; a particularly clear statement of it is found in his comments on strophes 13 and 14 of the *Cántico*: "en aquella noticia de la luz divina, echa de ver el alma una admirable conveniencia y disposición de la sabiduría en las diferencias de todas sus criaturas y obras, todas ellas y cada una de ellas dotadas con cierta respondencia a Dios..." This exercise, along with many others, is described in the Second Alphabet, along with instructions for practice and further information about the natural and spiritual worlds.

The Third Alphabet is concerned especially with *recogimiento*, or the *vía negativa*; in it also Osuna includes a great deal of information and moral counsel. The prologue to the First Alphabet, which introduces the first three, explains that each one imitates a Scriptural book that is also alphabetical. The First is compared to the lamentations of Jeremiah; the destruction of Jerusalem is represented, in Osuna's work, by the destruction of Christ's sacred body, brought about by the sins of the world. This Alphabet is planned to excite compassion and contrition. The Second describes ways of putting these sentiments into effect by beginning the spiritual reform of mental prayer. Such prayer may take the form of any of the spiritual exercises described. This Second Alphabet is compared by Osuna to Proverbs. The strong woman who is praised in the last chapter of Proverbs is identified by Osuna as prayer, whom the spiritual pilgrim must take to wife. The Third Alphabet traces its origin to Psalm 118, in which the sinless pilgrim is blessed: "Dichosos aquellos cuya senda es limpia, que caminan en la ley del Señor. Dichosos los que observan sus prescripciones, con todo el corazón lo buscan." Clearly, these Alphabets represent progressive stages on the road to perfection. In the Third, the soul actually sallies forth to the mystic encounter.

The Fourth Alphabet, promised in the Third, is an inquiry into why God is lovable, and why we are to love Him. Osuna lists seventy causes, which he has succeeded in abbreviating into the form of another alphabet. This one, however, is confined to a few pages (445-48); again, he says that it is intended as a memory aid. I see no reason to doubt his sincerity in this statement. Although the alphabetical format has its own mystic associations, a good memory is indispensible to the contemplative, and Osuna discusses this. The alphabetical organization does not determine the structure of the Fourth Alphabet. Rather, it follows the circular course of the Law of Love from heaven to earth and back again. Since it often deals with universal laws, much information about Osuna's science can be found in it. It contains much material for contemplation and meditation, particularly of the creatures. The book itself is an exercise, as is any devout preoccupation. One must read it with love and "go along reading and praying" (*4 Abc.*, 231). In this Alphabet, Osuna refers to Alphabets One through Three and to the *Norte*, saying that he does not wish to repeat in any book what he has said in another (*4 Abc.*, 401).

In spite of this, the Fifth Alphabet contains, in chapter 58, some material taken from the Third. Since this may have been the last work of Osuna's life, the question may be raised as to whether this late chapter, and perhaps succeeding ones, were added by another hand. Since the content of this book is so consistent with that of the others, I find it easier to believe that Osuna simply broke his own rule in this case.

The Fifth Alphabet is a *contemptus mundi*. The first part, labelled "consuelo de pobres," is intended principally for contemplatives, although the layman is also addressed. The second treatise, "aviso de ricos," is directed toward people in active life, with some special attention to prelates. In this Alphabet, texts are given in Latin (though often followed by translations), which suggests that a priestly audience was anticipated. Osuna was apparently told of the popularity of his works among the priesthood during the time of his residence in Flanders (de Ros, *Maître*, 608 and n. 3). Here,

Osuna's style is more personal, and he relates more of his own experiences and sentiments than in other works. In this book, too, he employs more frequently the opportune witticism, and also scathing social and moral criticism, some of it aimed directly at his priestly public.

The Sixth Alphabet is a treatise on the five wounds of Christ, according to a series of metaphors summarized in versets and arranged alphabetically. It is the most lyric of Osuna's works, although some strikingly poetic passages are to be found in all. The Sixth Alphabet contains a table, in Latin, of the scriptural texts cited in all six Alphabets and the *Convite*. It also has an index in it to each Alphabet and the *Convite*.

The works of Osuna reflect a progressive mastery of literary technique, and a few changes of opinion, but they remain essentially unified by the same fundamental concepts. Osuna traces the pattern of reality, as he sees it, through the moral, the physical, and the metaphysical worlds. In making manifest these several levels of reality, Osuna uses the figure as an important vehicle. The term "figura" is one he uses so frequently that its contexts define it clearly: it is a manifestation of reality that is accessible to the senses. Since to Osuna all sensible things are embodiments of spiritual reality, and the compendium of all spiritual realities is the Logos, then any created being may serve as a point of entry into moral or anagogical realms. The process is one of discerning the spiritual (abstract) nature of the object, be it rock, tree, animal, star, ship, or man himself.[17] To assist the reader, Osuna supplies a great deal of information about the world of nature and of man. However, he scatters these data throughout his works, and to collect all the significations of a creature requires some research. Thus his works themselves become an exercise in meditation and contemplation, as the reader carefully assembles the connotations he has learned of the terms in the passage he is reading.

---

[17] For an excellent discussion of the figure see Erich Auerbach, *Scenes from the Drama of European Literature* (New York, 1959), Chap. 1, "Figura." An interesting study employing somewhat different terminology is that of H. Flanders Dunbar, *Symbolism in Medieval Thought and its Consummation in the Divine Comedy* (New York, 1961), especially Chap. 1.

In his manner of composition, Osuna calls upon both the allegorical and the philological modes of Biblical exegesis, and his rhetoric can profitably be compared to that of the medieval preachers. Lynn Thorndyke remarked that students of literature have generally failed to work with the "similitudes" of things, which fill several important medieval collections.[18] These similitudes or analogies are an important aspect of Osuna's concept of the figure, and its use in the practice of meditation and contemplation.

Since any figure may have many characteristics, it can represent a constellation of spiritual realities. Therefore, the figure becomes a symbol into which is condensed a whole complex of abstract significations. These enrich a figurative passage with so many meanings that it becomes difficult to translate them into simple expository prose. In doing so, the translator must convert a set of simultaneous intuitions into cursive, analytical form. Besides the danger of falsification that attends this process, there is an inevitable loss of esthetic effect. Etchegoyen has directed our attention to this difficulty presented by mystical works in general, saying:

> L'étroit parallélisme qui unit la doctrine et l'expression de l'amour, les explique aussi l'un par l'autre. C'est en vain que les philosophes ont essayé de définir la premiére sans la seconde ou les littérateurs ont prétendu exposer celle-ci sans celle-là (Etchegoyen, *Amour*, 49).

For practical purposes this separation must, at times, be made. In the following chapters I have found it necessary to explicate at times the figure, at times the abstract principles it encarnates. Regrettably, the explications do not convey the emotive power of the figure; the image of a concrete entity is more likely to arouse emotion than an abstract explanation of it. Also, the figure

---

[18] Lynn Thorndyke, "The Properties of Things of Nature Adapted to Sermons," *Medievalia et Humanistica*, fasc. 12 (1958), 78-83. Some collections he names are: *Septiformis de moralitibus rerum naturae, Lumen animae,* and the *Summa de exemplis ac similitudinibus rerum* by John of San Gemignano. The article especially describes an anonymous fifteenth-century folio on the properties of natural things appropriate to sermons for the course of the year.

is a simultaneous presentation to the imagination, rather than a series of cursive propositions addressed to the intellect. An extreme example of the difference in effect between the two can be seen by comparing the poetry of San Juan de la Cruz with his own explication of it. The reader's reaction to the poem is quite different, I believe, from his reaction to the explication. Similarly, Osuna sacrifices esthetic values to his pedagogical intent in portions of his work. However, he inserts many passages in which explanations are lacking, or are incomplete, mutually inconsistent, or puzzling. This is intended to inspire the reader to meditate on the figures in order to see the images presented, to receive their emotive and esthetic effects, and to solve the problem presented. Osuna gives specific instructions as to how the reader should work; these will be seen in succeeding chapters.

Osuna was called by his contemporaries "el Crisólogo minorita" (Sarraute, *Vie*, XXXI, 40). The earlier Chrysologos had said that Christian doctrine was revealed in figures and parables so that it would be understood only by minds enlightened by the Holy Spirit.[19] Osuna follows the custom of using parables and figures, but he advises the reader to study diligently (*5 Abc.*, fol. 79). In most cases, Osuna's figures and their explications are so consistent that the careful reader can penetrate their hermeticism by the grace of the author's own assistance.

My purpose in this book is to supply the reader with enough data about certain figures and stylistic devices to enable him to perceive the effect of a difficult Osunian treatise. In the course of this, I shall have recourse to many of the author's own statements scattered through his works. When these statements are assembled, Osuna is seen to be one of the most communicative of the sixteenth century writers. His comments illumine not only his own writings, but also those of others.

Osuna's Castilian works include many pages of clear expository prose, often witty, sometimes hortatory, sometimes lyric. A virtuoso of literary styles, Osuna is important as a precursor of the later mystics, and it has been suggested by one critic that his

---

[19] Hugo Rahner, "The Christian Mystery and the Pagan Mysteries," in *Pagan and Christian Mysteries: Papers from the Eranos Yearbooks*, Ed. Joseph Campbell (New York and Evanston, 1963), 176.

influence is not confined to the literature of religion. Father Crisógono says in his study of Carmelite mysticism:

> Creo que una de las grandes injusticias cometidas con nuestros autores ha sido acordarnos tan poco de este insigne franciscano [Osuna], cuyos escritos no sólo fueron escuela donde aprendieron todos los más celebrados místicos españoles de últimos de aquel siglo, sino que va también a la cabeza de nuestra literatura de oro.[20]

How great Osuna's influence on secular literature may have been is yet to be determined. Certainly his information about the natural world and its abstract significations is very helpful to the student of Golden Age poetry. Also, his methods of meditation and contemplation show a clear relationship to the dialectics of *conceptismo*, as will be shown in a later chapter. As a moralist, too, Osuna comments on contemporary life, and these remarks reveal many facts about sixteenth century Spanish customs.

It has already been mentioned by Father de Ros (*Maître*, 277) and others that an exemplum used by Osuna in *El norte de los estados* also occurs in *Don Quijote*. I know of no evidence, however, that rules out a common source. It is possible, too, that Cervantes might have heard this anecdote from a preacher using Osuna's books as a source. However, Cervantes also uses, in *Persiles y Sigismunda*, the surname Villaseñor, which is the name of the interlocutor in *Norte*. In view of the popularity and wide distribution of Osuna's works, further attempts should be made to evaluate his influence on the literature of his century. Such efforts, however, are complicated by the fact that Osuna himself draws upon a large number of sources, some of which he does not name. The problem of ruling out common sources would be a substantial one.

The principal topic of this study is Osuna's use of figures in the dialectical and rhetorical structure of his works. But because these figures represent abstract concepts, it will be helpful first to investigate some of Osuna's ideas about the two abstract worlds — the

---

[20] Crisógono de Jesús, *La escuela mística carmelitana* (Madrid-Avila, 1930), 54. Cited by de Ros, *Maître*, 422.

Divine Ideas, and the mind of man. According to Osuna, the sensible and abstract worlds are analagous, and through meditation and contemplation these analogies can be perceived. The book that offers us the broadest view of these analogous realms is the Fourth Alphabet, subtitled the "law of holy love." From it I have extracted most of the material of the following chapter, which is intended to introduce the reader to some of the essential traits of this splendid sixteenth-century cosmos, where "God's goodness is written in the Scripture and painted in the creation" (*4 Abc.*, 238).

Chapter II

THE NATURAL LAW OF LOVE

The law of love is a natural law. Osuna explicitly distinguishes between *la ley positiva* and *la ley natural*. Positive Law "depende de la voluntad del que la instituye ... y porque la voluntad es libre, toda ley positiva es variable...." On the other hand, "la ley natural no depende de ninguna voluntad, ca por esto se dice natural, cuasi necesaria; porque ninguno puede negar lo que da la naturaleza; es tan necesaria la ley natural impresa en nuestra ánima, que el mesmo que la imprimió no puede revocar esta ley ni dispensar en ella..." (*4 Abc.*, 234). Natural law does not depend upon the will of God, but upon His intellect (*entendimiento*). By natural law He rules Himself; by positive law He rules all created things. Natural law is invariable, because the divine will coincides always with the rectitude of the divine judgment.

The first postulate of the law of love is that the good is to be loved, and the greatest good most greatly loved, for love is proportional to the goodness of its object. Second, it is affirmed that all things love the good; that is, the will of all things, created or uncreated, inclines toward the good. The good is the object of the will. In order that the will may be attracted to it, it must first be known. Goodness will be "tanto más amado por la voluntad, cuanto más conocido por el entendimiento" (*4 Abc.*, 236).

Is the good, then, anything that can be an object of the will? Osuna says that a thing "tanto tiene de bondad, cuanto tiene de ser" (*4 Abc.*, 237); "tiene tanto de bondad cuanto tiene de entidad y de substancia...." (*4 Abc.*, 236). Goodness, then, is proportional to Being. But created beings have goodness only as "añadidura o accidente," while the goodness of God is substantial, that is, while a man may *be* without being good, "nunca Dios puede ser sin ser bueno...." (*4 Abc.*, 237-38).[1]

We have, then, a situation in which the good is object of the will, and goodness is a correlate of being. Goodness communicates itself to the will through knowledge, but the will itself must act in this communication, that is, the *will to know* (*4 Abc.*, 503). Therefore it can be said that the will generates knowledge, which in turn inflames the will to love the goodness that is known. Infinite goodness, if it is known, must be infinitely loved. Since only God is capable of infinite knowledge, only He is capable of

---

[1] In short, goodness is predicated of the creature, but not of God, for all possible predicates of God are included in His substance. A predicate implies a quality, state, or action, all of which are considered to have no substance in themselves, but are attributes of substance. In God goodness is a substance, not an attribute; in the creature it is an attribute, not a substance.

To see the significance of this, let us compare two grammatically similar propositions: "the parrot talks" and "the lightning flashes." If we transform "the parrot talks" into a proposition of the type "some parrots talk and some don't," the result is both empirically and logically admissible. However, the same transformation of the second proposition results in "some lightning flashes and some doesn't," which is impossible, since the flash *is* the lightning. In this same way, Goodness is God; so is Love. In making this analysis I have found it helpful to refer to G. E. Moore, "Is Existence a Predicate?" cited by A. J. Ayer, in *Language, Truth and Logic* (New York, n. d.), 24-25; and to B. L. Whorf's statement about the classification of events as nouns or verbs in Hopi: *Language, Thought, and Reality* (New York and London, 1956), 215. The questions treated by these writers have features analogical to the problem raised by Osuna.

Note that the qualitites of God, since they are not to be attributed, will logically be taken as subjects; therefore instead of discussing attributes of God we more properly discuss His "names," which might also be called His "manifestations". This notion may be related to the theory of emanations that Osuna mentions (*1 Abc.*, fol. 99; *4 Abc.*, 351; *4 Abc.*, 513-14). On these last pages, Osuna says that all goodness is an emanation of God, and virtues "are a certain participation of God Himself sent to earth."

Osuna's idea that the properties of God are substantial seems reminiscent of St. Augustine's treatise on the consubstantial nature of mind, knowledge, and love (*On the Trinity*, IX. 4,5). The theory of emanations occurs in both Hebrew and Christian mysticism, and is, I believe, Neo-platonic. A complete study of Osuna's cosmology is yet to be made. Such a study might also have a bearing on the ideas of Fray Luis de León, who is also preoccupied with the Divine Names, including nouns that he, like Osuna, treats as figures (in *De los nombres de Cristo*).

fulfilling the law of love by loving infinite goodness infinitely. (In one sense, the rational soul can love infinitely; this will be discussed further on.)

The law of love is perfectly fulfilled in God Himself, whose "great name" is Love, although the name is especially applied to the Holy Spirit, which is the infinite divine will inclining toward the infinite divine goodness. Moreover, God is the substance or essence of love, as He is of goodness. Osuna here notes the difference between essence or substance and attribute, saying:

> ... por muy blanco que sea [uno], una necedad sería llamarle blancura, empero, como el amor que nuestro Señor tiene no le sea postizo ni lo tenga por manera de ornamento, sino que el mesmo Dios es fuente infinita de siempre vivo amor, — cosa muy justa es que le llamemos amor y le demos este nombre, por grande; pues grandes cosas anuncia de él. (*4 Abc.*, 292).

However, since the natural law of love is perfectly fulfilled in God alone, there is no apparent logical necessity for the creation of the universe. The Trinity is entirely self-sufficient without the Creation; why the troublesome material world was produced is a question that Osuna does not try to satisfy logically. He quotes Scotus, saying that God wished to share Himself with others who might accompany Him in loving His goodness, for their own benefit, not for His (*4 Abc.*, 245). He gave all things their natural being because of love; He always loves this being, although He may not love its works. If He should cease to love it, it would cease to exist. He creates things by naming them, "porque diciéndolo él, son hechas" (*4 Abc.*, 311). The Areopagite is also cited: "Salió Dios de sí cuando crió todas las cosas, según dice San Dionisio, a se les comunicar por amor, cuya propiedad es hacer que el que ama se dé al amado" (*4 Abc.*, 282). This is probably the best explanation, to Osuna, of the miracle of creation. When God "salió de sí," it was an ecstasy of love. Divine love is characterized by Dionysius as being "above reason,"[2] and he compares it to the passion of brute beasts, because of its violence and its irresistible and insatiable character. Osuna speaks of it as an

---

[2] Gabriel Horn, "Amour et extase d'après Denys l'Aréopagite," in *Revue d'ascétique et de mystique,* juillet 1925, num. 23, 282.

arrebato to which God is subject (*3 Abc.*, 454) as is the creature (*4 Abc.*, 461).

The universe was not created, then, because of logical necessity, since God fulfills all logical necessities within Himself. The only motive given for the act of creation is a passion — an ecstasy of love. Love is therefore the foundation of the universe, and is called by Osuna the "spiritual earth" on whose fruit we live. So that it can be seen to penetrate the entire physical world, he identifies it also with the other three elements. Love is water, which satisfies the thirst of our desire and produces holy thoughts as water produces fish; it is air which gives us the breath of life and helps us fly toward God; and it is fire, in which the salamander of charity is grown (*3 Abc.*, 498). Love put into effect brings joy (*4 Abc.*, 330), and God, Who alone can put it into effect totally, created the universe to share in this joy. The purpose or "end" of the creature is the same as its beginning; it is the fulfillment of love.

Osuna compares God to the sun, citing Dionysius: "Manifiesta imagen de la bondad divina es todo aqueste resplandeciente y sobreluciente sol." According to Osuna, the sun gives off both "operative" and "fecund" heat, which animate all things. This heat "entiende en la vida del hombre aun antes que sea el hombre, y entiende en la vida de todo aqueste mundo...." The heat that the sun sends forth is the same as the heat that it has within itself. This signifies that God loves us with the same love that He has for His own goodness. It is this love that engendered us, and because of this original grace — not because of our own merits — God loves us eternally (*4 Abc.*, 249).

The sun as a figure of God has many connotations pertinent to our considerations of the creation. Osuna believes literally in the sun's fecundative power: it engenders gold and precious stones in the earth, and fish in the water (*4 Abc.*, 261-62); it impregnates the earth (*4 Abc.*, 672). The old saying, "el sol y el hombre engendran al hombre" is interpreted so that the sun — God — and the Human Christ in His passion engender the just man who is to be saved (*1 Abc.*, fol. 24).

On the abstract plane, the sun is wisdom. The Word of God is the fount of wisdom; the sun is "sermón de sabiduría." "Sabiduría" is defined as "amor gustado de Dios." "El hombre sesudo permanece así como sol en la sabiduría (Eccli. 27: 12) que es amor gustado de Dios" (*4 Abc.*, 690). ("Amor gustado" refers to the experience of love in recollection; Osuna plays on the double meaning of the Latin *sapere*: to taste and to know.) The light of this sun is the Word because He illuminates the intellect. He is loving and wise (*1 Abc.*, fol. 62). God impressed into our souls the light of reason (*1 Abc.*, fol. 102). Light is also beauty; the beauties of all things are included in light (*2 Abc.*, fol. 151).

Heat, Osuna points out, causes growth in living things (*1 Abc.*, fol. 104). This aspect of the sun is often equated to the Holy Spirit, which also "dries up" carnal desires and "melts" the soul in compassion. However, the seven gifts of the Holy Spirit (wisdom, understanding, counsel, fortitude, knowledge, piety, and fear of the Lord) are all equated to effects of the sun (*4 Abc.*, 501-2). Similarly, Christ is depicted through different aspects of the sun (*4 Abc.*, 553). The rays of the sun descend to the earth to lift us, like water vapors, to Heaven (*4 Abc.*, 686), where we shall replace the fallen angels, just as water rises to fill a vacuum. The sun is taken as an image of the Trinity: the star itself is the Father, the ray is Christ, and from the two comes the Holy Spirit (heat) (*2 Abc.*, fol. 99). It follows naturally that the element of fire is taken by Osuna as a symbol of the Holy Spirit, and the attributes that are assigned to this element are explicated in spiritual terms at various points in the Alphabets. This fire that is the Holy Ghost has the property of being set alight by water, its opposite. (Water most commonly signifies sensuality to Osuna.) It is the baptismal water that ignites the flame of the Holy Spirit (*4 Abc.*, 360).

The sun of the human world is love (*4 Abc.*, 634), which is also equated to gold (*4 Abc.*, 503). Gold, we should remember, is engendered in the earth by the sun. Gold also symbolizes Christ's human body, engendered in the mortal flesh of Mary [as gold is produced in the earth by the sun] (*6 Abc.*, fol. 52).

Osuna's beliefs about the generative power of the sun are analogous to the alchemists' theory that the sun represented the masculine principle. Its terrestrial manifestation was gold. Correspondingly, the moon is a feminine symbol to the alchemists,[3]

---

[3] For a concise explication of these principles of alchemy, see John Read, *The Alchemist in Life, Literature and Art* (London, 1947), 7-10.

and to Osuna it frequently represents that which is human and, therefore, variable. It may signify the bloody flesh of Christ, the "moon in eclipse" (*1 Abc.*, fol. 88). It may represent our love, which is changeable (*4 Abc.*, 688); or our will, which reflects the light of knowledge (that comes from the sun) (*2 Abc.*, fol. 68), or our poverty compared to the largesse of God (*5 Abc.*, fol. 156). The moon beneath the feet of the Apocalyptic Virgin signifies carnal desire (*Norte*, fol. 7). The moon also symbolizes contemplation, because it is seen by night in the darkness of concentration. Here, the sun represents good works — thought brought forth into the world of action (*1 Abc.*, fol. 179). Just as Osuna sees in the sun a representation of God and the masculine principle of generation, there are suggestions throughout his works that the moon symbolizes mutable matter, a feminine principle incarnate in the Virgin. This postulate, however, is expressed principally in allegorical terms, some of which will be further discussed in later chapters.

Love: the unifying force. The properties of generation, light, and heat that Osuna attributes to the sun may symbolize all members of the Trinity, or any one of them. These properties may also represent the abstracts fecundity (the ability to generate beings or concepts), intellect, and will. Just as generative power, light, and heat are inseparable in the sun, the abstracts are inseparable in the Trinity and in the human soul. This, according to Osuna, is because of the nature of the will, generator of all intellectual activity, as will be shown in detail later on in this chapter. Love, a manifestation of will, has the catalytic property of transforming its subject and its object into itself. Thus, if you love God, you convert Him totally into love (*4 Abc.*, 240). Osuna cites St. Bernard to the effect that those who love become equal, and come to be one and the same thing (*4 Abc.*, 330). One of the important propeties of love is that the lover and beloved communicate in such a way "que se digan ambos uno, y esa mesma comunicación es amor" (*4 Abc.*, 308). But farther on he says that perfect love "no sabe hacer distinción entre el que ama y el amado" (*4 Abc.*, 326), although this seems to hedge the question of unification after a very positive assertion on the subject.

The problem may be a genuine fear of suggesting pantheism, since this natural law of love must apply to the relations between creature and Creator, as well as between divine Persons. Osuna vacillates on the exact nature of the transformation worked by love. His statements are boldest while he is speaking mostly of celestial beings, in the early chapters. But when speaking of man's natural ability to love God, he says, "El amor luego da entera posesión al amador..." (4 Abc., 407), which is a situation quite different from becoming, with the beloved, "una misma cosa." In fact, it clearly implies the subject-object relationship that has been negated by the concept that "el amor convierte en sí los suyos." [4] The logical consequence, pantheism, is sidestepped first by verbal quibbles: perfect love "no *sabe* hacer distinción entre el que ama y el amado," and "En el deseo hay una continencia *virtual* de las cosas deseadas" (4 Abc., 425. Italics mine). The question is taken up again with the same inconsistency: man is transfigured "en Dios" by love as iron is transformed and transfigured in the fire (4 Abc., 409). Fire, in any form, is a symbol of love; iron, however molten, is not fire. But the Holy Spirit is spoken of as fire, because it melts metals in order to unite them, "transformándolos en sí" (4 Abc., 355).

I believe that the body of discourse in the *Abecedarios* substantiates the view that Osuna's philosophy is not really pantheistic; too many of the figures preserve traits of essential difference between lover and Beloved. [5] Osuna may have had several reasons for offering seemingly incompatible statements. First, it is impossible for the contemplative to retain any consciousness of self in the state of ecstatic love; Osuna points out that this consists of complete forgetfulness of internal, as well as external, things (4 Abc., 461). The natural expression of such an experience may well sound pantheistic, and it is precisely this rapture that is Osuna's model for the union of God and the soul in love.

---

[4] A second meaning of *convertir* is exploited in the statement that love "convierte las ánimas al mesmo principio do el [el amor] salió" (4 Abc., 233). In the context, this seems to mean that it "turns the souls toward" the principle, or beginning, of love (that is, toward God). This is not the same as being converted *into* love ("el amor convierte en sí los suyos").

[5] Among the figures for the lover in the unitive state are *andas, arca, castillo, tálamo, templo*. The Beloved is the occupant of these containers. Also applied to this situation is the figure of the *esposa*, which presents us with the mystery of matrimony: two spirits in one flesh.

The difficulties inherent in depicting a state that consists of forgetting anything that can be *spoken* (*3 Abc.*, 352) may have forced Osuna into a definition by assertion and negation. Moreover, one of his rhetorical devices consists of making startling statements, which he then succeeds in reconciling to orthodox doctrine. However, on this important point, I believe that he is forcing the reader to make his own reconciliation, through the technique of analogy (which will be discussed at greater length in Chapter III). If both lover and Beloved are transformed into Love, it is not in the same "mode" of being — not, at least, when the subject and object are human and Divine. They do not become "equal" to each other, but rather analogous to each other. Both participate in one sublime operation: love. But they are like the same melody played in two different octaves. Osuna compares similar operations on the two levels, material and abstract, to voices singing counterpoint (*4 Abc.*, 221). Further on, he compares our imitation of Christ to a painter's imitation of nature (*4 Abc.*, 557). Since the natural law of love is binding on the whole material and spiritual universe, it will necessarily present the same configuration throughout, and all parts of the whole will be analogous to each other: all will seek their own good. But this will not make them all equal, by any means.

Because God contains all goodness, all things seek Him, and in doing so seek their own Source. The circle is the natural form of any exposition of Osuna's law of love, and this form will repeat itself, eventually, when almost any aspect of it is discussed. The Fourth Alphabet itself is so arranged that one circle is formed by the love of God for His own goodness, another by the reciprocal love between God and the angels, others by human love, and the great chain is finally linked again to its source when the pilgrim, man, reaches Heaven.

God, Man, and Angels. Goodness is not the only property of Being; another is Truth. These two correspond to forces found in rational beings — intellect and will. Each of these forces desires to unite itself with the appropriate property: goodness "demands" love; by the same line of reasoning, truth demands intellect (*4 Abc.*, 372-73).

Goodness itself has three *"maneras"*: *la honesta, la deleitable, la útil*. *La honesta* also appeals to the intellect (which, of course, can only detect it in the light of knowledge). The pleasing and the useful appeal to two aspects of the will — *la codicia* and *la potencia irascible* (*4 Abc.*, 690). All three aspects of goodness are totally contained in God. His desire, in creating the world, was that all should enjoy this goodness with Him: "ningún buen amor ama en tal manera sus cosas que las quiera retener sin las comunicar..." (*3 Abc.*, 319). God's wish, however, is all-powerful; it is immediately put into effect (*4 Abc.*, 524). Thus He wished us into existence according to the ideas in His own mind (the Logos); and by the same wish, that we might enjoy His goodness, He makes it available to us. On the material level, this may take the form of "fruits" of the earth, necessary to maintain the body. But in the spiritual realm, man is so created that God Himself can be attained by him, because his intellect has as much power to understand as God has to work (*3 Abc.*, 451), and his will can penetrate even where intellect does not reach (*3 Abc.*, 394). Between these two forces man is amply endowed with the ability to reach and enjoy, spiritually, the goodness of God.

The intellect, illuminated by faith [a good and correct understanding (*4 Abc.*, 408-9)] displays this goodness to the will, and the will by nature is inclined to it (*3 Abc.*, 348). The inclination of the will, which is desire, is the spiritual equivalent of the motion of a body through space. Osuna cites St. Augustine to this effect: "así como el cuerpo se mueve por algún espacio, se mueve el ánima por el deseo" (*3 Abc.*, 449). To awaken this desire by supplying knowledge is one of the objectives of the Alphabets.

It is, perhaps, worth noting that Osuna is aware of some aspects of the motion of bodies in space. He compares the inclination of the will toward the divine Goodness to the force of gravity, for example. He says:

> Aqueste amor consiste en un enderezamiento de la voluntad afectuosamente ordenada en aquel sumo bien, y tras esta voluntad, que es un acatamiento afeccionado á Dios, va todo el corazón y las entradas [sic] del hombre más prestamente que la piedra cuando desciende al centro de la tierra ..." (*3 Abc.*, 510).

And elsewhere he says:

> Hay tan amorosas y perpetuas ocasiones de permanecer siempre amando, según lo último de la potencia, que sería más fácil dejar de caer siempre una gran piedra que se echase en un pozo sin suelo, que dejar uno de los bienaventurados de amar al que les tiene el amor en peso puesto ..." (*4 Abc.*, 689).

Osuna seems to have put his finger upon the law of gravity,[6] and a part of the law of inertia. He states these as analogues to the spiritual motion, or "emotion," of love. It appears that he considers them both natural laws, and the spiritual movement, besides being analogous to the physical one, seems to him equally real. This attitude is one of the basic tenets of his philosophy; the soul in *recogimiento* actually moves toward God. It cannot do so unless desire lends it sufficient force to overcome inertia and all contrary impulses.

Rational beings, having free will, can initiate an action of their own. Thus they can elect either to follow the proper course of natural law, or to pervert natural forces to inappropriate ends. This last was done in the rebellion of Lucifer and in the fall of man, and this perversion of powers is held by Osuna to have had such cosmological effect as to dim the sun (*4 Abc.*, 260). The capacity of an organism to move freely in the direction indicated by the will seems to be a measure of spirituality. Any material body is hampered by inertia, whereas thought "like spirit, goes and passes wherever it wishes" (*3 Abc.*, 325). I believe that Osuna sees spirit as another and more subtle "mode" of matter, and thought or emotion another "mode" of passing through space.

This mechanistic view of spiritual events is also reflected in Osuna's methods of philological exegesis. A word may be explicated on its concrete, etymological level as well as on its

---

[6] Osuna's place in the history of science has not been studied, as far as I can discover. Here, he appears to follow an Okhamist (Franciscan) idea rather than an Aristotelian one. According to one historian, the Okhamist theory that both celestial and sublunary mechanics follow the same laws constitutes the dividing line between ancient and modern science. George C. Sellery, *The Renaissance, Its Nature and Origins* (Madison, Milwaukee, London, 1965), 177-79. Osuna displays such an interest in natural science that a complete study of his views might be worth while.

abstract one. In the following chapter, examples will be seen of such exploitation of levels in *ver, conocer, concebir,* and *alumbrar.* Latin and Spanish lend themselves readily to this procedure, because many abstract terms in these languages are based on concrete etymons. (This is, of course, true of many languages.) Osuna also turns to the Hebrew and Greek versions of the Bible, and explicates words according to their root meaning in those languages.

Although Osuna frequently makes humorous use of the double meanings of words, a study of his work shows that this progression from the concrete to the abstract is, for him, a serious and fundamental philosophical concept. He believes with St. Bonaventure that the activities of natural things show the workings of human psychology and of the Divine Ideas.[7] This belief is reflected also in his use of the figures; these are concrete objects, like the sun, that come to represent abstractions. Perceiving these abstractions is the purpose of meditation and contemplation of the creatures. The abstract or "spiritual" nature of the being reveals some aspect of the Divine. This notion is partially supported by Romans 1:20: "En efecto, las perfecciones invisibles de Dios, aun su eterno poder y su divinidad, se han hecho visibles después de la creación del mundo, por el conocimiento que de ellas nos dan sus criaturas ... ."

Since to love God is to collaborate with a natural law, Osuna points out that the commandment to love is really an invitation or "carta de amores" (*4 Abc.,* 437). It is an attempt to make a privilege appear to be a service, and a promise seem to be a demand. God wants us to enjoy Him: "se puso debajo de apariencias de pan y vino por nos enseñar cuánta voluntad tiene de nos inevriar á los pechos de su consolación" (*3 Abc.,* 458).

As this quotation suggests, love for God may permissibly be *codicia,* the desire for the pleasing. Osuna explicitly defends the propriety of "coveting" God,[8] supporting his assertion by a text from Ecclesiasticus [24, 25]:

---

[7] For a brief statement of this notion in St. Bonaventure, see Julius R. Weinberg, *A Short History of Medieval Philosophy* (Princeton, 1964), 165.

[8] Although he also speaks of the fire of evil *codicia,* which is sensual desire (*3 Abc.,* 347).

En mí está la gracia de toda vida y verdad, en mí toda la esperanza de vida y de virtud; acabad de pasar a mí todos los que me codiciáis, y sed llenos de mis generaciones, porque mi espíritu es dulce más que la miel, y la heredad mía más dulce es que la miel y el panal (*4 Abc.*, 268).

It is appropriate to love God with *codicia*, and also with *querer de amistad*, that is, the desire that the Beloved may have good things (*4 Abc.*, 267). The sin of Lucifer was that he loved himself with "querer de amistad," and coveted not the Maker, but His gifts (*4 Abc.*, 268-69).

As can be seen, one must observe proper order in love. While we are permitted to covet God for our own enjoyment (this joy is experienced in *recogimiento*), we are not allowed to covet His worldly gifts. In the "love of friendship," we are confronted with a paradox, for how can we desire "goods" for One Who has everything? The answer lies in free will, which was granted man (and angels) so that "de nuestra cosecha tuviésemos que le dar." We have nothing of our own to give Him, except our will or love, which He covets (*4 Abc.*, 389). Also, we must wish to endow God with the love of our neighbors, since He desires the love of all men. Love for neighbor therefore follows the same pattern as the love for God. We wish for others that they may enjoy the greatest of all "goods," the love of God, and eventual blessedness (*4 Abc.*, 535-37). In doing this, we try to give to God what He most desires, and we try to do the same for our neighbor.

"Neighbor" is defined as any man who can share with us in eternal life (*4 Abc.*, 531). Angels, too, are neighbors; we were created in order to fill the vacancies in their ranks after the heavenly rebellion. Both men and angels are governed by the same law (*4 Abc.*, 272). The angels are therefore enjoined to try to help us, and this accounts for their ministrations. Inanimate things also participate in compliance with the law: "things" will not permit a vacuum, in order that "no cese la comunicación y socorro que dan las causas superiores a las inferiores ni se corte aquella influencia común que desciende del cielo a la tierra." They also preach "communication" and largess: they give us alms (sheep give wool, water gives fish, the trees and the earth give fruit

(*4 Abc.*, 560). For our part, we can only try to repeat the process in the terrestrial sphere. In trying to achieve blessedness for ourselves and our neighbor, we make the angels rejoice, for we are rebuilding the heavenly city (*4 Abc.*, 507).

In this way we love our neighbors, angelic and otherwise, with the love of friendship. When it comes to coveting, we should covet their virtues; in doing so we make them ours (*4 Abc.*, 386). We may also enjoy their good counsels and companionship. Aristotle is cited as an authority on the proper nature of friendship, which Osuna summarizes as an effort on the part of each participant to conserve his own virtue and that of the other (*4 Abc.*, 541). It follows that we are obliged to conserve the virtue of our neighbor if we wish to see him attain a state of blessedness. To this end, we must first remedy the needs of those who, for want of food or other vital necessities, are in danger of committing a mortal sin (*4 Abc.*, 562). This duty takes precedence over all others, even that of contributing to religious orders. Laymen are obliged to help only the needy that they know of, but churchmen must seek out people in need of help.

Oddly enough, even popes and emperors never seem to have enough to give anything away, but under the moral law, he who has two pairs of shoes has one to spare (*4 Abc.*, 562-63). Ultimately, we are obliged to give our lives, of necessary, to save the soul of one wretched Jew, just as Christ died to save the souls of all sinners (*4 Abc.*, 554). It is also necessary to try to conserve the mortal life of our neighbor (and it is not sufficient to come with our assistance only when he is at death's door; then he needs God's help, not ours). To comply with this obligation we must, if necessary, accept financial ruin. The alternative is condemnation of the soul (*4 Abc.*, 561-63).

As can be seen above, love demands actions; it must be put into effect. "Hijuelos, no amemos con palabra ni con la lengua, sino con la obra y con la verdad" [I Jn. 3:18] (*4 Abc.*, 556). In imitation of divine love, we must make of our *afecto*, *efecto* (*4 Abc.*, 522-24). Osuna says (citing Hugo of St. Victor) that we must love with *beneficio* (*buena obra*), *palabra* (*sano consejo*), and *voto* (*piadoso deseo*). In this way we pay to our neighbor the debt that we owe to Christ (*4 Abc.*, 535), and imitate Him, becoming "perfect," not by equality but in imitation (*4 Abc.*, 548). Our copy is to Christ as a painting is to nature (*4 Abc.*, 557). Here be become analogical to Christ in our actions as we were found to become analogical to God by transformation into love. Love for others is the model of love for God: "Quien no ama a su hermano, que ve, ¿cómo puede amar a Dios, que no ve?" [I Jn. 4:20] (*4 Abc.*, 535).

The measure of love for others is love for self. "Ama a tu prójimo como a ti mismo." To love oneself with the love of friendship is to wish for oneself the grace of God. (Grace, to Osuna, is love.) In action, this type of self-love consists of giving oneself to God, and loving oneself for Him (*4 Abc.*, 509); since He has elected to cherish all men. The second type of love is to want Him for Himself (*codicia*), but "más graciosa cosa es dar [amistad] que recibir [codicia]." However, the two acts always accompany each other: "mi amado a mí, y yo a mi amado." The office of love is to bring God to us and us to God (*4 Abc.*, 509-10); love is "the unitive virtue" (*4 Abc.*, 507). Therefore, "giving" and "receiving" may also be equated to charity and hope — hope of His coming. Turning to the Greek root of *caridad* (*caris*), Osuna says it means "grace" (*4 Abc.*, 307), which is the beginning of love and the beginning (*principio*) of heaven (*4 Abc.*, 684-85).

Self-love. In self-love, as in other types, proper order must be observed. "El que ama su ánima la perderá" [Jn. 12:25]. To explain this, Osuna cites St. Augustine: "Si mal amares tu ánima, aborrecístela, y si bien la aborrecieres, amástela." This means that it is necessary to eliminate the animal inclinations of the soul: "más vale buena guerra que mala paz." We have to correct the animal body in order to subject it to the spirit; it is our "rebellious son" (*4 Abc.*, 511), or "our daughter who deceives us and deceives herself" (*4 Abc.*, 653). This is because the body's composition — the elements — works against the force of love. The element of fire produces wrath, which gives us a "swelling" that results in pride of spirit. Water, with its property of coldness, produces "tibieza," or "luke-warmness" in love. Earth, with its heaviness, ties us down to the things of the material world. There is no mention of air, probably because it is usually identified with spirit (*4 Abc.*, 694).

The body, nonetheless, is the instrument that we have to work with: it is "arma de justicia para la batalla espiritual" (*4 Abc.*, 511). It is mandatory to make it obey the will of the spirit. This is the *raison d'etre* of asceticism to Osuna. There can be nothing wrong with the body in itself, since God created nothing bad; it is only less good than the spirit. The first, or elementary, phase of the Christian life consists in detesting and overriding the impulses of the body when they contradict those of the spirit (*4 Abc.*, 513); sensuality must subject itself to reason. "Así como cuando este cuerpo terreno que tenemos está informado del espíritu vital, que es el ánima, se dice vivir, y no de otra manera, así cuando la sensualidad está informada é domada con las amonestaciones de la consciencia, se dice tener vida de gracia, según su posibilidad" (*3 Abc.*, 329). The proper relation between reason and sensuality is expressed as "la concordia de los hermanos, el amor de los prójimos, y el varón y la mujer que en bien consienten" (Eccl. V.c).[9] Sensuality is, of course, the woman: she is figured in Eve, and original sin consisted of the capitulation of reason to sensuality (*3 Abc.*, 333, 351).

When reason dominates, the fruit of its union with sensuality is good works (*3 Abc.*, 333). The "seed" is grace (*4 Abc.*, 255). Osuna insists always that good thoughts are not enough, nor good words; the body must produce actions to execute the aspirations of the spirit. Faith without works is dead; love without them is dubious (*4 Abc.*, 522).

> "El meditar no es otra cosa, moralmente hablando, sino un pensar cómo seguirás á Cristo; lo cual si no lo pones por obra, mejor te fuera no pensarlo, pues que, según dice Santiago, (Jacob. IV.d), por pecado se le cuenta al que sabe el bien y no lo obra" (*3 Abc.*, 520).

God, being One only, abbreviated all things in Christ, who in turn abbreviated all laws into the law of love (*4 Abc.*, 503). "El precepto mío es que os améis unos a otros, como yo os he amado a vosotros" [Jn. 15:12]. This love demands giving up one's life for one's friends, as Christ did. To know how Christ

---

[9] *3 Abc.*, 330. Sic. The quotation is actually from Ecli. 25.

loved, we must look at His works: "las obras que yo hago en nombre de mi padre, éstas están dando testimonio de mí" [Jn. 10:25]. God demands of us only love, but this consists of external works as much as of internal affections. Since man is composed of body and soul, his works have two aspects: terrestrial and divine. These consist of action and prayer. Lifting the hands in prayer signifies readiness to join action to thought, as St. Francis recommended (*3 Abc.*, 474-75).

One figure representing love is "el oro encendido y probado." Love is gold because it enriches us spiritually; it is fiery when there is a genuine interior passion; and it is "proved" when it is put into action. Actions, for their part, engender love: "de la manera que los hábitos se crían con los actos, así el amor se cría y engendra con la obra" (*4 Abc.*, 523). Thus love is both cause and effect of action.

Since all laws are comprehended in the law of love, Osuna shows how each of the Ten Commandments can be interpreted in relation to it (*3 Abc.*, 503-504).

From this brief sketch of the action of love in the universe, we can see how it comprehends morality, asceticism, and theology, which last is seen as a correct undestanding of reality. Data about these may be conveyed through dialectics, the Scriptures, or spiritual exercises consisting of mediations. All these find a place in the *Abecedarios*, but it is important to remember that all of them serve the same end — they are fuel for the flame of love. Asceticism in itself has no value whatever for Osuna; its only function is that of breaking the domination of the sensual nature over the spirit. Virtue comes off somewhat better, but to practice virtue for its own sake is to advance no further than the pagans.

A knowledge of theology, or of the natural world, occupies a peculiar position in Osuna's works. Intermittently he voices the platitudes of "docta ignorantia," and at times in all seriousness he gives examples of saintly people who are unlettered. In such cases, he says that God Himself has been their teacher, but he counsels against depending on such instruction in one's own case. At every turn, the reader is advised to exert himself as much as possible, for his comprehension of the limitless God will be small enough at best, and one must know Him to love Him.

However, part of Osuna's work is a purposeful engima which requires for its solution a great deal of information about theology, and about nature as he conceived it. Perhaps he followed the tradition of hiding the more arcane parts of his doctrine from the vulgar eye. On this subject he again expresses himself in contradictory terms: well he knows that the doctrine of *recogimiento* is not suitable for everyone (*3 Abc.*, 320), but later he announces that men and women, religious and secular, are invited, one and all, to participate (*3 Abc.*, 401-02). To resolve this contradiction, I believe we should turn to Christ's words: "quien es de Dios, escucha la palabra de Dios" [Jn. 8:47]. Christ's parables were understood only by those already endowed with comprehension. "For whosoever hath, to him shall be given" [Mat. 13:12].

However, Osuna counsels his reader to depend less on natural or divine endowments of intellect than on sheer work. In the case of meditations, he says that they must be read twenty times, committed to memory, and "revolved" in the mind as though they were to be taught to someone else (*5 Abc.*, fol. 8). Since his meditations contain a great deal of information, anyone who has learned one or more of them in this way has already proved the inclination of his will, at least. The popularity of Osuna's books indicated that his method must have produced results.

Learning is, however, only a means to an end, and so is the delight of *recogimiento*. Osuna's purpose is to teach the Christian life. All information, exercises, and moral precepts lead to the principle of love of God, neighbor, and self, expressed in action. The Christian must try in every way to imitate the life of Christ, who is the Mirror of God and the Archetype of man. Osuna admits that every individual has a different capacity for perfection, but he contends that everyone is able to transform himself up to the final limit of his capacity — which, he believes, can grow constantly until death. The source of this marvelous capacity for change is the will, the fountain of love.

The will. Osuna holds that the will is a force of nature. Indeed, it is the primary one, for without it there would have been no creation. This explains why the Holy Spirit, elsewhere defined as the divine Will or Love, is also called *Potencia*. The will is the active principle, and it has, naturally, two aspects —

"querer y no querer." For this reason the "fountain of love" is said to produce sweet and bitter waters (*4 Abc.*, 266-67). "No querer," says Osuna, is always based on a desire for something else that is not compatible with the rejected item. In determining what is to be desired, and what rejected, the will works within itself, with the co-operation of the intellect alone. Osuna describes this operation as "como un abrir de ventana para que vea qué ha de ser hecho" (*4 Abc.*, 503). This appears to be a likeness of the primary exercise of perception and judgment. Based on this glimpse of things, the will then commands the other powers (intellect and memory) to act in accordance with its decision (*4 Abc.*, 503). It may command the intellect to acquire knowledge, or the memory to present its records.

Because it dominates the intellect, love is called "honorable sabiduría." Its effect is to illuminate; for this reason it is called, in the Scriptures, fire. The Holy Spirit came in tongues of fire; that is, it inflamed (with love), and instructed (*3 Abc.*, 512).

This sketch of the will's function appears to agree at most points with statements by St. Augustine. Augustine says that inquiry, or the desire of finding, precedes knowledge, which is a thing "uttered and fashioned." The will finds the knowledge and conjoins it to the mind. Will, therefore, has temporal priority over knowledge; it is the desire by which knowledge is conceived and brought forth. It holds and embraces its offspring, knowledge, and unites it to its begetter, mind (*On the Trinity*, IX, 12.).

Since the three powers of the soul are memory, intellect, and will, it is fairly easy to progress from the will as "parent" of knowledge to the will as "parent" of the soul. Without it no mental effort would take place, and knowledge would not be conceived by the intellect nor stored by the memory. Osuna calls the will the "mother of the soul" (*3 Abc.*, 454).

We can also see now why Osuna says that the will can penetrate where the intellect cannot; we may desire knowledge that we cannot "utter and fashion."

In another sense, too, the will may be said to be the mother of the soul, because it is through the affirmative will of God that the soul comes into existence. Should this affirmative will cease, the soul should necessarily cease to exist (*4 Abc.*, 311), because the will of God is immediately executed. The possession of life is therefore a guarantee of His continued attention. (Since God's memory is total and perfect, once we are willed into existence we persist in His mind as ideas forever. Hence we are immortal [3 *Abc.*, 442].) His will constitutes a sort of unbreakable connection between the individual and the Source of all being. It is within our power to find this original juncture, because in the very desire to find it there is "a virtual containment of the thing desired."

Every will can produce love according to its force and the magnitude of the thing that it loves (4 *Abc.*, 351). For example, we love the sun more than an ordinary star (4 *Abc.*, 239). Proper order must be observed in directing the will; the original sin consisted of placing secondary things first. The will itself is only a force, and as such is morally neutral: it is good or bad according to its object (4 *Abc.*, 624). Everything in creation is less good than God, therefore the desire for anything other than God is a falling-away from perfection. In Osuna's philosophical scheme, the only room for evil lies in failure to select the highest good, because of error in intellect or will, or in lack of sufficient resolution to follow up the decision. The operations of the devil in the world consist of deceits and distractions, as well as temptations. (See the Third Alphabet, Treatise VII.)

The ordinary cause of our lack of perfection lies in another attribute of the will: it is changeable. It cannot rest long without loving something (Origen is cited) (4 *Abc.*, 416). It fills itself with whatever is put before it, like a mirror (4 *Abc.*, 244). This accounts for the role of spiritual exercises; in one way or another they display the knowable features of God to the will, so that it can become enamored of Him. It is the duty of memory to present this image constantly (4 *Abc.*, 377).

Reason tells us that the will should naturally incline toward God. First it is natural that the part love the being of its Whole more than its own being. In nature, this is observed when water rises, contrary to its nature, because it is "vencida por la inclinación de todo el universo que se ha de conservar. ..." It rises to prevent a vacuum, which would disrupt communication between the natural orders, in which resides the good of all matter.

In the microcosm, the hand and arm will risk themselves to protect the head. (There are two meanings here: Christ is the head, and Christians the members, of the mystical body.) Even the snake will defend its head with its whole body. Osuna quotes St. Thomas Aquinas to the effect that the natural inclination of irrational things shows the natural inclination of our will. (See *4 Abc.*, 403-04 for this paragraph and the preceding one.) Again, the material world is shown as an analogy to the abstract.

Since man is a participant in the divine Goodness, he naturally loves the Whole more than himself or any other part. If this were not so, natural love would be perverse, and infused love (grace) would have to destroy human nature, whereas in reality it perfects nature. The gifts of God to the soul are like medicine to the sick: they reduce it to its natural state of wholesomeness.

We naturally desire the ultimate perfection, blessedness, for ourselves; we want it above all things. Since God is the source of blessedness, we love Him above all things (*4 Abc.*, 404).

In the love of the part for the whole, and the coveting of blessedness, Osuna has reiterated the two types of love mentioned earlier — *querer de amistad,* and *codicia.*

Natural reason also shows that the greatest good must be most greatly loved, and the will can correspond to what the intellect shows it. As an example, Osuna says that a mistaken man can love a "criatura" above all things and enjoy her with his own natural forces. In the same way we can love God and enjoy Him with these same natural forces. The will conforms to the truth just as it conformed to the lie. As a final proof that we can love God above all things with only the help of natural endowments, Osuna points out that if it were otherwise, we could know when we were in a state of grace, which is inadmissible (*4 Abc.*, 405).

As the above paragraph suggests, the course of love is the same whether the object is human or divine, and both loves lead to generation, of a sort. (In the case of divine love, it is knowledge that is conceived.) Osuna freely utilizes the traditional vocabulary of human love — the "pelea de amor," "cerco de amor," "cautiverio de amor," "cárcel de amor," "herida de amor," for example.[10]

---

[10] Osuna mentions in the Fourth Alphabet (543) both *Celestina* and the *Cárcel de amor.* He deplores them, which hardly proves either that he has or has not read them. The allusion to the "criatura" here could be suggested by *Celestina,* but this is not necessarily the case, of course.

Since natural forces alone enable us to love God above all things, it follows that even the philosophers, with a good intellect and the "general favor of God" could do so (*4 Abc.*, 403). This is almost certainly a reference to pagan philosophers, since, to Osuna, that is the usual referent of the term. Osuna holds that, since the beginning of the world, "sibilas y profetas y adivinos" meditated on the Passion, and the philosophers frequented *recogimiento* (*3 Abc.*, 483). Osuna says, however, that infused love reinforces human love, and also refines it, making it like gold instead of copper (*4 Abc.*, 403). Osuna does not say whether natural love alone was sufficient to win Heaven for the philosophers or not, but he strongly suggests that it was (*5 Abc.*, fols. 186-87).

Three conditions are necessary to natural love: these are a pure heart (purification of thoughts and desires), a good conscience (good works), and faith (a good and correct understanding) (*4 Abc.*, 409-09). There is always a possibility of error in intellect, and this is fatal to the enterprise of love, for if your concept of God does not accurately represent Him, you will not find Him (*4 Abc.*, 410). This passage is interesting, not only because it shows that love demands a complete domination over all aspects of life, but also because it implies that God is found either in, or through, the concept.

Another source of error is the will. For example, we might wish that God would not be just, in our own case; we would prefer mercy. This is the wish of the sinner, and we must renounce mortal sin before we can hope to love God above all things (*4 Abc.*, 411).

Natural love and grace. This natural love is the most perfect act we can perform with our own forces alone. It is the perfect way to seek God, to go to Him, and to "convert ourselves" to Him. This love is the ultimate disposition that the soul can make, by its own efforts, to receive grace (*3 Abc.*, 492). (Such a disposition can be made even in a soul that has at some time incurred

---

Osuna makes an interesting suggestion about the pastoral genre when he says that in Hebrew the word for "pastor" may also be interpreted as "amador" (*4 Abc.*, 345). See my article, "An Etymological Basis for the *Pastor-Amador* Equation," *Romance Notes*, XI, 2 (Winter, 1969), 368-71.

mortal sin.) When this love is in the heart, grace is immediately infused, "porque cuando el sujeto está dispuesto con la última disposición que se requiere para la forma, luego inmediatamente se infunde la forma" (*4 Abc.*, 406).

The loving soul, it appears, is in the feminine situation [11] of matter seeking form. The act of receiving it is grace. This form is infused in the mind; the "ser de gracia" is received in the rational part of the soul (*1 Abc.*, fol. 102). For further details, see Chapter III. What the new form may be is shown by the following gloss:

Osuna says that "Imperfectum meum viderunt oculi tui" (Psal. 138b) is read in the original Hebrew as "Informe meum viderunt...." He explains this as meaning that to our poverty, "cosa informe," God will give the form of Christ.[12] God always supplies what is lacking (*5 Abc.*, fol. 23). With the infusion of grace, man is transfigured "en Dios por afición entrañal," as iron is transformed and transfigured in the fire (*4 Abc.*, 409). The new form is that of the Perfect Man. But this transformation is worked through the concept, "seen" in the mind's eye. It is not a corporeal image; the soul cannot communicate to the senses its spiritual vision (*2 Abc.*, fol. 108).

Grace, which is necessary to achieve this summit of contemplation, is infused love, given to us "gratis." There are two types — one that makes us pleasing to God, and another that makes us useful to others — a special ability to preach, for example (*3 Abc.*, 440). Grace is the beginning of love; without it we could not love God (*3 Abc.*, 449). This seems to imply that the pagans who loved God above all things had received grace; I have found nothing in the Alphabets to make this appear impossible. The desire for God is a gift from God, and we can be sure of having already received one grace if our heart is moved by this desire.

---

[11] For some further comments on this notion, see C. S. Lewis, *The Allegory of Love, a Study in Medieval Tradition* (New York, 1958), 90. Aristotle's theory was that the female contributed all matter to the offspring; the male all soul or "form," Charles Singer, *A Short History of Anatomy and Physiology from the Greeks to Harvey* (New York, 1957), 24-25.

[12] A further exposition of this new infusion of form, which Osuna considers a "re-generation," will be seen in succeeding chapters.

God is like the *pregonero* who sells wine. He gives the first sample free, but the rest has to be paid for (*3 Abc.*, 328).

Osuna plays on different meanings of *gracia* (*3 Abc.*, 437). He also points out that we love those that are *graciosos*, and those that we love seem to us *graciosos* (*4 Abc.*, 306-07). This is the nature of grace, divine or human; once the creature is loved it has grace. (Compare the attitude of San Juan de la Cruz, *Cántico*: "Ya bien puedes mirarme / después que me miraste / que gracia y hermosura en mí dejaste.") We receive God's love only because of the merits of Christ; through Him grace came to us.

Grace and charity are both types of love: charity is specifically divine love, and grace is infused love. Grace can be called hope because it is a foretaste of heaven; "una gota de miel del panal de la Gloria" (*3 Abc.*, 372).

Grace supplements natural love, and by its action awakens free or "deliberate" love. Natural love, which we have discussed, comes from God and is always present (*3 Abc.*, 510); it is basically self-love, although it may rise to sublime heights. Deliberate love follows knowledge. When both loves seek the same object, the whole man is caught up by their impetus (*3 Abc.*, 510). Grace is as vehement as natural love, says Osuna, citing St. Ambrose (*4 Abc.*, 398). When the two loves coincide, their object is soon attained, and the result is joy (*gozo*) or delectation. The "interior" and the "exterior" man take delight in God: "mi corazón y mi carne se gozaron en Dios vivo." This joy is both carnal and spiritual; it is attributed to the heart and the flesh (*3 Abc.*, 510).

To Osuna it is quite natural that both flesh and spirit should enjoy union with God. To have held otherwise would have been inconsistent with his own thesis that the law of love operates similarly in both spirit and matter. Pursuant to this thesis, Osuna affirms that married people can love God above all things, and can practice *recogimiento* (*3 Abc.*, 401-02). Philosophically speaking, the only thing wrong with carnal love is that it represents disloyalty to Divine Love, which demands undivided attention. Visible things of any kind are an impediment to Divine Love, because "nuestra poquedad no puede juntamente á todos" (*3 Abc.*, 321).

When natural and deliberate love join forces in loving God, man is returned to his original state of innocence. Osuna quotes Gerson: "Bienaventurado es el que su libre amor conforma al amor natural, porque si dos consintieren, ser les ha dado del Padre celestial todo lo que pidieren, ca no pedirán sino á Dios o conforme á Dios y á la naturaleza que fué primero instituida" (*3 Abc.*, 510). That is to say, the spirit and the flesh are again united, like "varón y mujer que en bien consienten."

Corazón y ánima. Spirit is contained in the heart and is therefore identified with it. The body is represented by *ánima*, or that part of the soul that is sensual, i.e., animal (see Chapter VI for further discussion). These are identified with the *pájaro* and the *tortolica* of the Psalm (83): "Porque el pájaro halló casa para sí, y la tortolica nido donde torne a poner sus pollos." The bird is the heart; the turtledove the flesh that contents itself with only one spouse (*3 Abc.*, 510-11).

When our love is both natural and deliberate, we love with *el corazón* and *el ánima*, the abstract and the sensual aspects of the soul. However, in citing the commandment "Amarás al Señor Dios tuyo con todo tu corazón y con toda tu alma y con toda tu mente, y con todas tus fuerzas" [Mk. 12:30], Osuna reads *alma* as *ánima*, and *mente* as *memoria* (*4 Abc.*, 438). Although memory is properly a function of *corazón* and *ánima*, he reiterates it here, either because he is using a different version of the Scriptures, or because of the importance that memory has for him.

Love of heart, soul, and memory correspond to the three virtues of faith, hope, and charity. (The heart is the source of mental activity, and faith is a correct understanding.) Hope corresponds to *ánima*, because "la esperanza anima" (*4 Abc.*, 377-78). (This explanation seems frivolous; can it be that the correspondence depends on the idea of matter "hoping" for form?) Charity, the greatest of the virtues, is reserved to memory, for several reasons. One of these is that the constant memory of God is, in Osuna's opinion, the highest spiritual exercise of those he mentions. It presupposes *recogimiento*, and is called by him a "resurrection" after the "death" of extinguishing the senses. On less advanced levels of contemplation, it is a thought that one is in the presence of God, and "un inquirir con viva solicitud del corazón, que apenas se olvida de lo que busca" (*3 Abc.*, 445).

God's memory, like ours, is a book, in which are found the essences and ideas of all individuals (*3 Abc.*, 442). This memory must, I believe, be the Logos.[13] Osuna calls Christ the open book that shows all things (*4 Abc.*, 278).

To love with the whole heart means to apply the four passions (joy, sadness, fear, hope) to love (*4 Abc.*, 443-44). Osuna explains: You must enjoy love; joy is the most noble passion, and the one that conforms best to our risible nature. This is the only passion that we shall retain in Heaven. Sadness should occur only when you feel your love diminish in fervency. As for fear, the only fear you should have is that of losing love. And love has a better hope of being favored by God than any other virtue, because it is the greatest. The passions may be represented by the four wheels of Elijah's fiery chariot, in which he was lifted from the earth.

It is evident that the passions, like the will, may be applied well or badly. They provide motive power to send the soul on its flight to the Divine. The passions are all functions of the will (see Chapter VI) and share with natural love the task of providing the animal force necessary for this strenuous enterprise.

Osuna never fails to stress the necessity for vehemence, impetus — excess in love. The rigorous mental and physical discipline that he recommends is designed to channel all energy, and all attention, toward one object. Love of God is the only virtue in which there can be no excess (*4 Abc.*, 436-37). Although we can never know God totally, our love for Him can increase indefinitely; in this sense it can be said to be infinite (*4 Abc.*, 385-86). Often the desire to love God infinitely "overflows," and the soul is enraptured into an ecstatic state (*4 Abc.*, 434).

We must teach ourselves to love readily and intensely. All the things that naturally provoke us to "mal amor" (songs, beautiful things, perfumes, flowers, music) should be used as an incitement to love God (*3 Abc.*, 510). The Canticle of Solomon is used to teach the sublimation of carnal love (*4 Abc.*, 634-35).[14]

The intensity of passion prescribed by Osuna is difficult to attain and to maintain, and apparently requires both courage and tenacity. He repeatedly emphasizes the necessity of both, and the

---

[13] Compare W. R. Inge, "Logos," *Encyclopedia of Religion and Ethics* (New York, 1951), VIII, 133-38.

[14] This idea appears also in Origen. See Anders Nygren, *Agape and Eros* (London, 1953), 388.

power of love to override all obstacles. Love does not turn back "aunque la razón y la imposibilidad le sean contrarias." (Osuna cites Richard of St. Victor, *4 Abc.*, 427). It is daring: "ni demanda juicio, ni se templa por consejo, ni se refrena con empacho, ni se sujeta con razón; ruego, suplico, demando: Béseme con el beso de su boca" [Cant. 1:1]. (Osuna cites St. Bernard, *4 Abc.*, 398.)

The natural law of love endures in man as long as he endures, even though he be in Hell (*4 Abc.*, 234-35). This is one reason why fire is the chosen symbol of love; fire never loses its property of being hot as long as it exists, although all the other elements may change their properties. For this reason also, the Holy Spirit came in the form of flame. In addition, the different aspects of fire (light, flame, heat, the sun) lend themselves very well to identification with Divine Persons, and to such ideas as "inflamed" love, or the "illuminated" mind (which "gives birth" [*alumbra*] — to knowledge). Moreover, the nature of flame is to rise, and the flame of love "lifts our spirit" (*4 Abc.*, 441). Several Scriptural texts lend support to the identification of fire with love. Among these are Deuteronomy 33:2,3 which is quoted by Osuna as "ley de fuego está en su mano diestra, y él amó los pueblos" (*4 Abc.*, 285). Osuna says that Christ is fire, and He heats the earth (man, created from clay), until the earth is changed into the fire of love, a substance resembling the substance of Christ himself. Thus he interprets the text (Sal. 143:5): "Toca los montes y humearán" (*4 Abc.*, 321).

Love endures even after the death of the body: "Tan fuerte es el amor como la muerte, y dura es, así como el infierno, la persecución" [Cant. 8:6] (*4 Abc.*, 264-66). Osuna adds that, like death, it pardons no one (*4 Abc.*, 344). The law of love is to be obeyed even at the cost of life, as Christ obeyed it. Love separated Christ's soul from His body, which death could not have done (*1 Abc.*, fol. 63). His love proved stronger than death, and He arose entirely transformed into spiritual Man. The Christian is urged to "die" also to the carnal man, and to come forth again as a spiritual being, an imitation of Christ. This is, in effect, a new creation stemming from the same source as the original one: from love made manifest in action.

Chapter III

MEDITATION AND CONTEMPLATION:
CONCRETE AND ABSTRACT

The Alphabets of Osuna are designed, as has been said, to induce love of God through knowledge of Him. He is a world unto Himself, which can only be investigated through reference to the second world, His creation, made in His image (*traslado*). Both these worlds are abbreviated in man, who, because he lacks knowledge of the Divine, cannot know himself. His remedy is to consider the second world (the created universe), in order to know himself and to be able to return to his Source (*2 Abc.*, fol. 131).

Knowledge thus acquired falls into one of two classes: it is either *sabiduría* (spiritual doctrine) or *sciencia* [*sic*] (a lower form, the doctrine applicable to the active life). Knowledge, or "doctrine," must precede works (*2 Abc.*, fols. 124-125). This knowledge is gained through spiritual exercises; these are the "words of God," and it is necessary to learn the *primeras letras* (*3 Abc.*, 460).

This is one fundamental reason for Osuna's choice of title for the *Abecedarios espirituales*. Typically, he does not explicitly identify it as his reason; rather, he gives other, relatively minor motives for his choice. He says that the simplicity of his genre reminds him of his humbleness, and that he is imitating Jeremiah, David, and Solomon.[1]

---

[1] *1 Abc.*, fol. 5. The Lamentations of Jeremiah and Psalm 118 are still arranged according to letters of the Hebrew alphabet. Since Osuna on one

Man, in order to return to his source, must not only love God, but must make himself fit for the celestial company. Man enjoys the unique privilege of freedom to make himself what he will. Osuna says that God left us "half-made," and to each person "le dió poder que se acabasse y se pintasse y dibuxasse como quisiesse, al talle y medida que por bien tuviesse" (*2 Abc.*, fols. 101-02).

---

occasion interprets the significance of a Hebrew letter preceding a verse by Jeremiah, he may be aware of symbolic values attached to alphabetical letters, and they may have influenced the structure of the works. This matter offers material for another study. The Alphabets are compared to Jacob's Ladder. However humble they may seem, "from small plants grow great trees."

In view of Osuna's interest in natural science, it may be significant to compare Plato's statement that some call the four elements "letters" of the universe, "whereas one who has ever so little intelligence should not rank them in this analogy even so low as syllables" (*Timaeus*, transl. by Francis M. Cornford [New York, 1959], 47).

In Hebrew, the word for truth is *Emeth,* written Aleph, Mem, Thaw. Aleph and Thaw are the first and last letters of the alphabet. Truth was considered to be the highest of all God's perfections. To this word, therefore, was attributed a mystical meaning: in God "truth dwells absolutely and in all plenitude." It also signified that God has neither predecessor nor successor; He is the beginning and the end.

Apparently this alphabetical idea passed into the early church, where the Greek Letters Alpha and Omega were substituted for the Hebrew Aleph and Thaw. However, the Greek word for "truth" does not end with Omega, so that the signification "plenitude of truth" was lost; the idea of "beginning and end" remained (The Catholic Encyclopedia, s.v. *Alpha and Omega*).

Considering the encyclopedic nature of Osuna's works, the idea of "truth...in all plenitude" seems the most adequate explanation for his choice of an alphabetical format, and for his use of the term "letters" to designate whole bodies of knowledge arrived at by dialectical processes.

The apparent coincidence between some of Osuna's ideas and the Hebrew tradition, his references to the Hebrew Bible ("la verdad hebraica"), and his generous use of Hebrew etymologies, raises the possibility that he may have been a convert from Judaism. If so, it becomes understandable why we have no record even of his family name. This might also account for the official silence surrounding his tenure as *Comisario* of the Franciscans in the Americas. This possibility remains to be explored.

Osuna, in one passage, utilizes the numerical value of letters to extract an allegorical meaning. In this case (*4 Abc.*, 273) he refers to Greek letters, and cites a gloss. Gematria is generally associated with Hebrew, but both Greeks and Latins used letters as numerical signs, and the practice was continued in the early Church (The Catholic Encyclopedia, s.v. *Alphabet*).

Each man takes the semblance that pleases him most. He can leave one form to take on another. "Su costumbre hace diversa la pintura: dará su corazón a la semejanza de la pintura: y velando acabará la obra" (Eccli, 38.c). Some, through the habit of vice, come to resemble devils; others seem to "conform" to beasts. The lion represents pride; the serpent, avarice; the pig, "las inmundicias de la lujuria" (*2 Abc.*, fol. 101). (The quotation from Ecclesiasticus refers to those who engrave figures on seals; the art will be referred to again.)

But man is made in the image of God; he is a participant in the Divine nature and capable of divinity. This image is so clearly impressed into his soul that it makes that soul immortal. But "el hombre como estuviesse en honra no entendió: fue comparado a las bestias insipientes y fecho a ellos conforme" (Psal. XLVIII.b) (*2 Abc.*, fol. 101).

Obviously, man can perfect himself by modeling himself according to the Divine Image in his own soul. In order to "see" it, however, he must have recourse to the created world, and of all created beings, the Human Christ is the perfect copy of the Creator. Osuna says:

> ... el Padre Eterno se figuró [en Cristo] muy al proprio ... con el pincel de su intelligencia: y sacó la figura tal qual era lo figurado perfectissima sin falta alguna; y esta figura no pienses que se distingue ni se señala con rayas o colores ni otras qualesquier señales como las que hacen los pintores que no pueden figurar la cosa sino conforme a los accidentes y aparencias que d'fuera parecen ... (*2 Abc.*, fols. 108-09).

The Son is a figure of the substance of the Father, but has the same essence. This figure is invisible; it was hidden under the

---

Among Franciscans, there may have existed already a traditional association between the alphabet, the totality of truth, and God. This idea is to be seen at least as early as Tertullian (see Chap. V, n. 1). Américo Castro (in *La realidad histórica de España* [México D.F., 1962], 434) says:

> Preguntado San Francisco por qué recogía los escritores paganos con la misma solicitud que los cristianos, respondió que era "porque en ellos encontraba las letras de que se compone el nombre de Dios...Lo que hay de bueno en esos escritos no pertenece al paganismo ni a la humanidad, sino sólo a Dios que es el autor de todo bien" (Castro cites from a secondary source).

figure of man. The second figure covers the first (*2 Abc.*, fol. 109). Its purpose is to make God visible to men, so that they can see Him and "conform" to Him (*2 Abc.*, fol. 103).

Although Osuna never declares clearly how the invisible God is to be seen in the visible Man, the process can be inferred. Osuna says:

> ... podríamos tener cuasi en todas las cosas memoria de Dios si atribuyésemos á El más que á las mesmas cosas las operaciones que ellos hacen, y pensásemos sernos hechas del mesmo Dios, pues que según su verdad lo son ... ni por eso has de pensar que Dios es forma de las cosas, aunque según verdad sea más necesaria su cooperación á las cosas para que obren que no la forma á la materia para que tenga ser ... (*3 Abc.*, 443-44).

Although this seems somewhat mysterious, it is further clarified by the statement that the doctrine of Christ is seen, not in words, but in His actions (*1 Abc.*, fol. 21). "La ymagen de Jesu Christo ... es la vida trabajosa y llagada que viuió..." (*6 Abc.*, fol. 53). Generally, the image of God that Osuna sees in created beings is to be found reflected in "las operaciones que ellos hacen." For example, Christ is called the "great Eagle" because of the following attributes: the eagle is solicitous of its young, making a nest in the heights to avoid the danger of serpents (the nest is the Evangile). The eagle provides its young with the blood of live victims (*1 Abc.*, fol. 105), so that they will be braver and stronger (Christ's provision of the Eucharist) (*1 Abc.*, fol. 125). Moreover, if the eagle sees that its young are in danger, it carries them on its shoulders to a safe place (the Redemption). It tests its children, to see if they are really eaglets. It pecks at them to make them leave the nest (tribulations — my interpretation), and it sets an example for them by flying. Christ's arms, extended on the Cross, are the wings of the Eagle flying to the heights of martyrdom.

If the eaglets do not fly, the eagle stops feeding them, provoking them to seek their own food. (Osuna says that this represents Christ leaving his disciples, so that they would learn to fly in contemplation, in which the soul flies from the nest of the body.) Its wings are faith and love.

The eagle flies so high that it is lost from sight. Christ flies to the "heaven of Deity" and cannot be seen in this life, "sino por los antojos claros de la fe." "Sale de quicios de hombre e pone su quicio e su nido e su assiento en Dios." (Osuna uses word-plays freely, both for serious purposes and for comic effect.) As God, He flies very low, "abatido en la humildad." He is first, in Deity, and last, in the humility He follows. His wings are mercy and love.

Continuing with his "declaration" of the eagle, Osuna says that its eyesight is so excellent that it can look at the sun without blinking. The sun is God; Christ the Man was unable to know (*conocer*) all divine things simultaneously, but He could know them successively.

The eagle, from the sky, sees the little fish swimming in the sea. When they come close to the shore, he descends and catches them up to take them to shore. The fish are Christians, the shore is Death. The allusion is to Christ's role as guide to the dying, the subject of the tilde in the Second Alphabet.

The eagle renews itself: in old age it loses its feathers and with the new ones it is rejuvenated. Christ lost his "plumes" (life and honor) in the Passion, and in the Resurrection he was renewed. "Vuestra juuentud señor sera renouada assi como la del aguila" [Ps. 102].

The eagle is the queen of birds, as Christ is superior to angels. Angels are heavenly birds that fly in contemplation (*1 Abc.*, fols. 105-08).[2]

Pliny is cited to the effect that the eagle is very swift because it is hot. This heat is love (equivalent, we recall, to motion) (*5 Abc.*, fol. 53).

Almost all these comments on the eagle form a "declaration" of the first words of the passage "una águila grande y de grandes alas con larga distancia de miembros llena de plumas y de colores vino al monte líbano: y tomó la medula del cedro, y lleuóla a la tierra de canaan, y púsola en la ciudad de los negociadores" (Ez. 17a) (*1 Abc.*, fol. 105).

---

[2] In the *Kitab al-mi'raj*, or *Liber Scalae* of Mohammedan mysticism, angels have the form of eagles. Mahmoud Manzaloui, "English Analogues to the *Liber Scalae*," *Medium Aevum*, XXIV, 1 (1965), 332.

The rest of his exegesis is, briefly, as follows: the eagle's size is emphasized to show Christ's superiority over the saints, who are often figured as eagles in the Scripture. Lebanon ("incense"), to which the eagle first came, is the soul of the Virgin, where Christ was first conceived; the cedar is her body; the "medula" represents "las más puras sangres de la virgen que eran lo mejor y más secreto de su persona assí como la medula." The pleasant odor of cedar represents virginity, which is pleasing to God. Canaan signifies "mercader"; that is, Christ, who "bought" (redeemed) us. Heaven is the "casa de negocios," populated by angels who go up and down on the business of the militant church. Carrying up the "medula del cedro" is a figure of the Ascension. (*1 Abc.*, fols. 105-106).

We can see in Osuna's treatment of the eagle how knowledge of the divine world is found in contemplation of created things. In the first place, the form, material and color are not so critical as actions, relations with other things, and the position of the creature within its category. (There is some correspondence here to Aristotle's concept of form and definition as correlates to function; this will be discussed further. Traditional notions of the eagle's performance are appended to the Scriptural text in which it is mentioned; both are taken as statements of scientific fact.

According to Osuna, the gall of the eagle is used to make a lotion to clear the eyes, as the Passion and blood of Christ permitted Longinus to "see the light."

The eagle is strong of foot, beak and wing. Christ makes nests for us in His hands and feet — in His wounds that devout people (eagles and turtle-doves) meditate. Christ's mouth represents the Word, which is sufficient to defend us from all harm.

The eagle is very hot and dry, and has the lightest and most ardent heart of all birds. When it sits on its nest, it imprints its nature most on the egg nearest its heart, and this chick most resembles its mother. Therefore, St. John the Evangelist was more truly a son of Christ than the rest of the disciples. When, at the Supper, he was received on Christ's breast, he was warmed and transformed into a great eagle, imitator of Christ, for "without delay he was conceived in the heat of the Holy Spirit" (*6 Abc.*, fol. 55). This is Osuna's explanation of St. John's traditional symbol.

Osuna applies his data about the eagle to the activities of man, the third world. Here, the eagle is the contemplative, who provokes his children to fly: that is, he teaches the art of contemplation. *Recogimiento* is the nest, the *arrebato* is flight, and the contemplative even loses sight of himself (*3 Abc.*, 400).

The eagle examines its young, turning them toward the sun to see if they can look at it without blinking. Thus the contemplative examines his intentions and desires, and casts out those "que no se enderezan al sol" [Dios] (*3 Abc.*, 423). In Glory, our souls will be able to look at God without blinking, because of the great quantity of light in our own eyes at that time (*3 Abc.*, 348, 350).

The eagle perseveres longer in flight than any other bird. Like an eagle, we can fly lightly through the contemplation of the creatures, toward Him alone (*3 Abc.*, 586). The reference to "God alone" is to the essential God, beyond form or categorization.

Other attributes of the eagle are exploited: "muchas aves siguen al águila cuando ha de repartir lo que le sobra de su caza, mas al trabajo de la caza solo se halla." Here, the other birds are those who follow Christ in times of spiritual consolation, but who refuse to suffer as He did (*3 Abc.*, 520).

The eagle may even represent the devil. The eagle blinds the deer by loading his feathers with dust and shaking them over the eyes of the animal, which being blinded, falls. Thus the demon brings to the contemplative evil thoughts that blind him (*3 Abc.*, 393).

It is in this manner that Osuna applies his information about the created universe to the two unknown worlds, the Divine and the human. Natural law — in this case, the activities of an animal — is taken as an indication of the trajectory of invisible or "spiritual" forces. These indicators delineate the figure "que no se distingue con rayas o colores." Such vectors, or courses of action, are shown to be parallel in the three worlds, and give rise to Osuna's comparison of meditation to counterpoint (*4 Abc.* 221), and the statement that his First Alphabet is a "subtle" song (*1 Abc.*, fol. 3).

In the dedication of the Fourth Alphabet (221), Osuna says:

> Sobre los ojos, nos dió nuestro Señor el entendimiento para que cantase contrapunto sobre el canto llano de las cosas visibles que se nos ofrecen y, dado que a vuestra señoría [3] como a todos, ofrezca Dios la universidad de las criaturas que son guiones [4] que llevan el entendimiento al que las crió ...

Osuna describes the course followed by the intellect as it meditates upon the creatures. He says that if you are walking by a field, and intend to use it as your topic, you should forget its particular characteristics and work from its "general name," so that "your meditation will be more free" (*2 Abc.*, fol. 137).

Related to this is the statement that we do not contemplate visible things but invisible ones, "porq̃ las visibles temporales son, y las que no se veen son eternas" (II Cor.: 4d) (*5 Abc.*, fol. 8).

In the perfect contemplation of *recogimiento*, the imagination does not function, "sino sola la inteligencia que buela sobre lo imaginable, hasta el mesmo Dios, donde el amor sube" (*3 Abc.*, 508).

In the last passage, we see Osuna's use of the term *inteligencia* in the context of pure contemplation. Intelligence, to Osuna, is a specific function of *entendimiento*, the general term for the intellectual faculty. Osuna defines intelligence as follows (citing Richard of St. Victor):

---

[3] The dedication is to Francisco de los Cobos, secretary to Carlos V.

[4] *Guion*, according to the Academy Dictionary of 1734, "en la música es la nota ò señal que se pone al fin de la escála, quando no se puede seguir, y ha de volver à empezar, y esta señal denota el punto de la escála, linea ò espacio en que prosigue la solfa." Covarrubias: " ...se llama guión una virgulita torcida en el cabo del renglón, que señala en qué lugar ha de estar el punto de la otra regla o pauta, que se le sigue." It appears from these definitions that the *guion* marks the key of the next canon or the next repetition of the old one. As a form of *guía*, *guion* and *guiona* occur in Berceo (Rufino Lanchetas, *Gramática y vocabulario de las obras de Gonzalo de Berceo*, Madrid, 1900, 393. Since the term "guiona" is applied to the Virgin (*Milagros*, 32) it may be construed in the context as "spiritual guide."

Abbot Suger of St.-Denis (1081-1151) remarks of an allegorical window installed in his abbey that it is "urging us onward from the material to the immaterial," *A Documentary History of Art*, ed. Elizabeth G. Holt (Garden City, N.Y., n.d.), I, 33.

... la inteligencia ve las cosas invisibles de Dios, no como las ve la razón, que investigando y discurriendo por los efectos y causas viene á conoscer las cosas ocultas y absentes como si las viese; no desta manera, sino como solemos ver las cosas corporales con la vista corporal visible y corporal y presencialmente, ansí la inteligencia pura para mientes á las cosas invisibles invisiblemente, y acata presencial y esencialmente las cosas espirituales, conosciendo que no están ligadas ni presas con apariencias de fuera; de manera que cuando el hombre no cura de la imaginación que rebuelve cosas corporales, ni de la razón que suele andar discurriendo de unas cosas corporales á otras para investigar las espirituales, sino que representa delante de sí a Dios purísimo espíritu desasido de todas estas cosas que parecen, y se detiene en aquel apurado acatamiento sin discurrir a otra cosa, entonces se dirá que usa de la inteligencia (*3 Abc.*, 566).

The faculty of intelligence, then, has the characteristic of working with abstractions alone, and it does not go discursively from one concrete object to another. It is compared to ocular vision, I believe, because of the immediacy and simultaneity of concepts presented by the intelligence, as opposed to the discursive, and less intimate, findings of reason. The distinction corresponds to one often drawn between intuitive and logical knowledge. (It should be recalled that Osuna has said, in speaking of the eyesight of Christ the Eagle, that as Man He could not know all things simultaneously, although discursively he could. Obviously, simultaneous knowledge is considered the higher form, and characterizes the Divine. It is related, perhaps, to the timeless "present tense" in which Osuna sees all the abstracts projected.)

Recalling Osuna's instructions on meditating, we see that the field, for example, must be divested of its individual characteristics and reduced to a "general name" — that is, it is removed from the category of concretes to that of abstracts. This "frees" the thought from particulars, so that any attribute applied to "fields" in general may be considered, whether they are appropriate to this particular instance or not. Also, any Scriptural passage referring to the concept may be used; we have witnessed this procedure in Osuna's treatment of the eagle.

The imagination, which deals with particular images, is useful to "reason," because it supplies the particular objects that are the raw materials of discursive thought. Reason, therefore, occupies an intermediate place in this theory of knowledge. The abstracts that it formulates are collected by the intelligence into simultaneous presentations. The faculties of imagination and of reason may profitably be compared with Aquinas' *species intelligibilis impressa* (the mental image), and the *intellectus agens*, or creative power that "shines upon the sense data, and makes them ready to produce a knowledge in which reality is deprived of all its concrete and individual features." It is this power that enables us to abstract the idea of "two-ness" from the particularized sense-impression of two horses or two coins. [5]

In his declaration of the eagle, Osuna undertook, he said, to show the reader how to meditate the grandeur of Christ in a creature. The attributes of the eagle that he chose to emphasize were principally its program of action. When Osuna compares each pattern to its analogue in the divine or the human sphere, he must abstract the formal characteristics of the pattern in order to do so. The process is similar to that of writing a formula for a sentence, without regard to the specific noun, verb, or other lexical item involved. In isolating the canonical pattern, however, we have produced an abstract similar to the one represented by musical notation; it is a pattern of form without concrete content. Although it is an abstract, it is not a simple one like "beauty" or "loyalty," but rather a composite that operates through time.

In using a noun like "eagle," Osuna may exploit any of the patterns that he has attached to it. Therefore, the single word will be treated, not as a concrete term, but rather as a cluster of abstract canons. The word, in juxtaposition with others, presents

---

[5] Maurice de Wulf, *The System of Thomas Aquinas* (New York, 1959), 23-25. Although the intellectual faculties distinguished by Aquinas do not correspond to those of Osuna, the process of abstracting generalities from particulars is clearly isolated here.

Osuna's instructions for meditation are closely related to Aristotle's description of induction (proceeding from particulars to universals) and for "reasoning by similarities" (seeking similarities between things and between their names, which helps to establish the definition of a genus) (G. M. Le Blond, *Logique et methode chez Aristote: Étude sur la recherche des principes dans la physique Aristotelienne* [Paris, 1939], 31-39).

to the mind the canons that they all have in common, plus some individual ones. These are voices of the "counterpoint" sung by the intellect over the "canto llano" of visible things.

To use another comparison, Osuna treats a significant word like "eagle" as though it conveyed one or more parables, not as an allegorical figure in our usual sense of the term. (The allegorical figure is ordinarily an entity that represents another entity; the eagle represents patterns of action.) He may be aware of the common etymon of "palabra" and "parábola." In one instance, he uses "palabra" with the meaning, apparently, of "sentence" (*1 Abc.*, fol. 77). Defining "palabra," Osuna calls it a thought or "razón" formed in the heart (*3 Abc.*, 569).[6]

Osuna's figures are words whose canonical patterns are used to represent the functioning of the invisible. Anything in Scripture or in nature may become a figure, as soon as its attributes are perceived. Even relatively inert materials may serve; their "operations" will consist of their physical or chemical properties.

Any figure may be composed, like that of the eagle, of canons established by Scripture, tradition, and observation. Osuna cites many authorities: Pliny, numerous philosophers both Christian and non-Christian, and glosses for preachers. These are mixed with the natural science of his day, bestiary lore, the literary tradition, and other material that probably comes from Christian apocrypha, folklore, and actual observation.

As a result of this mixture, the canons associated with any given figure are, to us, unpredictable. Osuna remarks on the intellectual freedom enjoyed in meditation of the creatures (*2 Abc.*, fol. 129). Content depends on information available to the meditator, and his selection of the canons he wishes to pursue. In the case of the eagle, Osuna has supplied many of these rather systematically, in the First Alphabet, for the expressly stated purpose of demonstrating how to meditate. In the Third Alphabet, however, where the eagle is referred to only through his analogical relation with the contemplative, the pattern is never systematically

---

[6] Compare Juan Pérez de Moya, who translates *logos* (in etymologizing *tropológico*) as "palabra, o razón, o oración" (*Philosophia secreta* [1st ed. 1785], Madrid, 1928), I, 10. Since a "word" may be a complex concept, the letters that compose such words may carry more significance than the modern reader might suppose.

given, and must be supplied by the reader's memory and rational inferences. Most of the figures used by Osuna are never explicitly drawn in such detail as that of the eagle. The reader must remember bits of information scattered by Osuna throughout the series of his books.

Speaking of meditation, Osuna says:

> Los que más útilmente piensan dentro de sí las cosas de Dios, se fortalecen más en la fe por la nueva lumbre de verdades que hallan en la meditación y sanctos pensamientos, así de las escripturas de las criaturas é artes de los hombres inventadas. Estos muchos se aprovechan de la lumbre natural é sentidos interiores del ánima, abriendo bien los ojos del corazón, que son las noticias é conoscimientos de las cosas, y escuchando y parando mientes en las correspondencias de los misterios, é hablando, esto es, argumentando dentro de sí, deduciendo y sacando unas cosas por otras, é trayendo muy convenibles congruencias y provaciones para mejor conocer (*3 Abc.*, 348-49).

In his instructions on meditation of the creatures, Osuna says that one must refer some things to others, and compare one thing to another as is done when meditating the Scriptures. Sometimes this is difficult, and it is necessary to disinter wisdom as though it were a treasure buried in the ground. This type of contemplation consists of knowledge about the "creatures." Besides moral doctrine that inflames the will (in love), one can acquire "speculative doctrine" that enlightens the mind (*2 Abc.*, fol. 130).

The process of referring, comparing, and deducing could well describe the search for canonical forms, conducted by discursive reason. The first stage of this activity — extraction of the canons from visible objects seen in the imagination — he usually refers to as "meditation." When the question is one of manipulating the canons alone, the term used is "contemplation," which he also applies to intuitive perception whether such perception has form or not.

Osuna's use of these terms corresponds to that of Richard of St. Victor, who named three types of spiritual exercise or mental prayer: *cogitatio, meditatio, contemplatio*. In the first type, mental images and figures are of material objects; in *meditatio*, reason seeks the hidden truths, and in the third, only invisible things are contemplated.[7] In Osuna and in Richard, it would appear that contemplation is distinguished from meditation by its exclusion of the visible. This leaves an ambivalence in the term "contemplation;" it may refer to the manipulation of abstracts, or to the state of *recogimiento* in which all categorization is suppressed, i.e., where everything is excluded that could be put into words.

Osuna himself identifies the Fourth Alphabet as an example of the use of the creatures to acquire a knowledge of God.[8] However, all the Alphabets share this trait. They are compounded of materials for cogitation (clearly stated doctrine, descriptions of Hell, the Passion, the Last Judgment, the agony of death; all to be taken literally), and materials for meditation. The reader may rise to the higher level of contemplation whenever the context, and his own resources, allow him to do so. (A great deal of his success depends on his memory of the canons of things; in this the "parable-word" is a distinct aid, since it provides a whole set encapsulated in one term.) Osuna, by oblique reference to hidden canonical forms, or by juxtaposition of different figures having an unexpected canon in common, forces the reader to attempt the manipulation of pure abstracts, which is contemplation. An extensive example of this technique will be found in chapters VII and VIII.

---

[7] Paul Dudon, "Le livre de l'oraison mentale du P. Melchior de Villanueva (1608)," *Revue d'Ascetique et de Mystique,* Num. 21, janvier 1925, 51-59. Villanueva (ca. 1547-1607), clears up the ambivalence of the term "contemplation" by distinguishing four types of mental prayer of the intellectual type (there is also prayer of the will). He calls the combination "a choir of four mixed voices."

[8] " ... determiné que sería perfecta oración referir todas las cosas a su Hacedor, y aun las divinas, sacando de ellas amor y amando por ellas, como por medio, al que las crió ... Pues mi negocio en este libro no es sino tratar dende lo más alto hasta lo más bajo y buscar en todo el amor de nuestro Señor Dios, que como luz resplandece en todas las cosas ... " (*4 Abc.,* 231).

Chapter IV

THE EAGLE DESCENDS: INCARNATION OF THE WORD

It has been seen that the Scriptural passage about the eagle was treated as another canonical pattern. It was used here, however, as a figure of events in the Evangile (the Incarnation, Redemption, and Ascension). This corresponds to Osuna's statement that the Old Law (the passage is from Ezechiel) is a figure of the New (*4 Abc.*, 288). However, we have already seen that the Divine Humanity itself is a figure of the Divine Spirit; that is, the permanent patterns of operation, or canons, must be discovered behind the historical figure of the Man. This means that the contemplative should attempt to penetrate the mystery of the perpetual incarnation of the Word, its power to redeem and to return the believer to Glory.

In this enterprise, it is necessary to refer to yet another figure used by Osuna: the important one of generation and birth. This is a figure of his theory of knowledge. Osuna says, citing St. Augustine, that knowledge ("noticia y conocimiento") engendered in the mind is its "fruit"; "del objecto y de la potencia se pare la noticia." He also quotes St. Paul to the effect that we cannot have a good thought of our own; if any should occur to us, it is engendered and infused by God into our minds (*1 Abc.*, fol. 14).

The soul's capacity to formulate knowledge is produced in its turn by the Word, Who gives to the soul the light of reason. The mixture of this light with His is life (*1 Abc.*, fol. 102). Also, the Word of God is Love; and is the *simiente* by means of which God is born in the heart.

In the preceding chapter, it was shown that an ordinary word may have, for Osuna, the force of a parable or group of parables. Such a word is "el Verbo de Dios," elsewhere called "Sermón de Dios" (*4 Abc.*, 527), "Tablas ... en donde el padre escribió todas las cosas" (*1 Abc.*, fol. 116). Deity is in Christ under the name of "libro" because the Son receives it by way of the intellect. He is called a book because He is "Noticia viva y engendrada del Padre" (*2 Abc.*, fol. 139). He is "llena de las razones formales de todas las cosas" (*1 Abc.*, fol. 102).

The Word of God is apparently the sum total of truth, which was abbreviated into a parable, the life of Christ. But "the science of this Book is not discursive; rather it is learned immediately upon being seen" (*2 Abc.*, fol. 138). The Divine Word corresponds, then, to simultaneous knowledge generated by pure intelligence, rather than to the successive presentations of discursive reason.

In God, this knowledge is engendered unceasingly, as indicated, Osuna says, by the present tense of the verb in "mi padre obra...." He notes that the present tense is used to indicate "un ahora invariable." (*2 Abc.*, fol. 36.) This is a statement of linguistic fact. Any assertion that is assumed to be an eternal truth will ordinarily be stated in the present in Spanish: "Dos y dos son cuatro."

In engendering Christ, God gave the power of generation, both corporal and spiritual, to all things (*4 Abc.*, 314). "Spiritual generation," in man, can only be generation of knowledge. The intellect of man is made fecund, mysteriously, by the power given to the Word. The role of love in this process (cf. Chapter II) is again suggested by Osuna's identification of the affections as "los oídos del ánima" (*4 Abc.*, 341).

The act of knowing Osuna designates by the verb *conocer*, which may have the Biblical significance "have carnal knowledge of," just as the verb "to know" in English. In this act, the intellectual power and the object conjoin to produce knowledge. Knowledge thus conceived, if it changes the actions of the knower, is brought forth into the light of material reality; that is, the mind gives it birth (*alumbra*).[1]

---

[1] The following passages show some of Osuna's varied uses of these terms:

Osuna's theory of knowledge, which includes love as an important element, follows admirably the parable of corporal generation. The relation between the two is that of the abstract to the material. Double meanings of *conocer, concebir,* and *alumbrar* form parallel vehicles for expression of the figure. Its extensive use is fortified by St. Augustine's reference to the role of love in the "conception" of knowledge (*On the Trinity*, IX. 12), on the three types of words — one is "knowledge together with love" (*On the Trinity*, IX. 10), and his comparison between the Incarnation of the Verb and perception of Him is the mind (*On the Trinity*, IV. 20).

An important reinforcing element is the Canticle of Solomon. Hatzfeld points to its influence in the literary expression of bride-mysticism in sixteenth-century Spain.[2] Undoubtedly it is an important factor. Another that must be considered is the terminology of the Augustinian theory of knowledge, borrowed by Osuna and extensively developed. Also, the Aristotelian theory that matter was essentially feminine and spirit masculine served to place carnal humanity in a feminine relation to the Divine Spirit. The nuptial figure is particularly apt, since it suggests the role of love in the process of knowing, and also the creative nature that Osuna attributes to the act of conceiving an idea. In addition to embodying two major philosophical ideas, the nuptial figure has the power to evoke sentiments and sensations. This is one of the avowed purposes of Osuna's rhetoric (see Chapter V).

The name "Aaron" ("el que concibe"): Osuna says that he is a figure of the good Christian, who, for the purpose of improving his life, conceives of God in his mind (*2 Abc.*, fol. 125).

Honor and blessedness of the soul consist of the "sight" of God and "conocimiento amoroso suyo" (*2 Abc.*, fol. 108).

"El ánima intelectual, con un abrazo cuasi incorpóreo de aqueste Dios uno, se hinche y empreña de las virtudes ..." (*4 Abc.*, 512).

To women about to give birth, one says "Dios os alumbre." The motive for this is that Christ may send mercy through His mother, whose name means "alumbradora" (*Norte*, fol. 86). (Elsewhere, Osuna gives different meanings for the name of Mary.)

In the Third Alphabet (348) Osuna says: "La fe es lumbre para alumbramiento de las gentes ..." (here, context makes "illumination" the most likely meaning).

[2] Helmut Hatzfeldt, "Die Spanische Mystik und ihre Ausdrucksmöglichkeiten," *Deutsche Vierteljahrschrift für Literaturwissenschaft und Geistesgeschichte*, Halle, 10 Jahrg. Heft 4 (1932), 625.

Osuna's views on the creative power of the mind penetrate his most fundamental doctrines. The "ser natural," he says, is received in matter (corporal conception); the "ser de gracia" (re-birth of the Christian) is received in "the rational being" (the mind). The Word is the source of both these lives (*1 Abc.*, fol. 102).

Referring again to Ezechiel's passage on the eagle, it is now apparent why Osuna specifies that Mary conceived Christ in her soul (her mind), which he identifies with Mt. Lebanon. The mountain, to Osuna, may be a figure of the contemplative (*3 Abc.*, 345). The Incarnation of the Word, and the advent of the concept to the contemplative, are both figured in the eagle's descent. His flight to Canaan, on this level of interpretation, becomes a figure of the contemplative's spiritual resurrection and salvation.

Alumbrar, ver, conocer. One of the eagle's attributes most emphasized by Osuna is its ability to see well. In his declaration of this point, Osuna interprets the eagle's ability to look into the sun as representing Christ's complete knowledge. This point is clarified by reference to Osuna's theoretical explanation of vision; it is made possible by light within the eye mixing itself with light from outside. I shall cite a part of Osuna's statement, which bears on our topic:

> Para mayor declaración de aquesto es de notar que para ver y conoscer las cosas corporales no basta la lumbre de nuestros ojos, pues de noche, á oscuras, aunque tengamos los ojos abiertos, no vemos; mas es menester que entrambas estas dos luces se mezclen, la luz de fuera y la que está dentro en nuestros ojos se han de juntar para que en la tal mezcla veamos las cosas visibles; así en lo espiritual es menester, para que se cause conoscimiento, que con la lumbre natural que está impresa en nuestra ánima se junte la lumbre divina y celestial, para que en esta mezcla veamos lo que antes no conoscíamos y podamos decir con David [Psal. XXXV]: En tu lumbre, Señor, veremos lumbre (*3 Abc.*, 348).

Sight is only possible when the disproportion between internal and external light is not too great. Bats and owls are blinded by sunlight, because the quantity of light in their eyes is relatively small. "Según el filósofo, la cosa sensible, cuando es muy excelente en su genero, corrompe el sentido...."

The intellect follows the pattern of the eyesight. Because our understanding is relatively limited, we can never reach the Divine through rational processes (meditation). The only recourse is through the highest type of contemplation, "no pensar nada," where all categorization is suppressed, and the Divine is not "seen" but "embraced" (*3 Abc.*, 348-49).

The Eagle, Christ, because of the light within His intellect, can know all things; that is, He has sufficient light in His own eyes to look directly at the Sun (God). Christ Himself is identified with the light from the Sun, "porque alumbra el entendimiento" (*1 Abc.*, fol. 62). *Alumbrar* is probably used here in both its senses, since the Word creates, as well as illuminates, man's mind [as the sunlight engenders gold in the earth, and fish in the sea]. The words "alumbrar" and "conocer" have meanings that permit them to be used in the figure of birth as well as that of sight, both of which represent the act of knowing.

In order to see a thing, we must first have some idea of it. "Para que veamos alguna cosa es menester que tengamos primero en nosotros su semejanza mediante la cual puede ser vista por nosotros." (*2 Abc.*, fol. 103). (I believe that Osuna may be noting here the difference between an undifferentiated sense-report and the mental perception of an entity from this report.) Also, "la noticia intuytiva" perishes in the absence of "lo que por ella conosciamos;" or, if God absents Himself, we lose Him from our "sight" (*2 Abc.*, fols. 107-8). This is consistent with Osuna's statement, seen in Chapter II, that the "noticia" is born of the object and the mental power. The problem, for which I have yet to find a satisfactory explanation, is how the omnipresent God may be "absent." If the object of the intellectual power is taken to be an impression in the mind itself, however, this absence can be explained as a lapse of memory or of attention (*tenerlo a uno presente*). Osuna insists on the importance of attention on the part of the contemplative; "attention to Him alone" is the "eye" of the soul, which wounded the heart of the Spouse (Cant. 4: c) (*5 Abc.*, fol. 57). Also, the apparent "absence" of God might result from a false impression of Him; Osuna has already called this an insuperable obstacle to finding Him.

It is the "noticia intuytiva," or presentational type of knowledge that is sought in contemplation. This type is probably represented when the eagle is said to look at the sun without blinking, that is, the entire view may be encompassed at one time without any discursive shifting of attention from one part to another. This is the type of knowledge that creates the "picture" mentioned in the Ecclesiasticus text cited in the previous chapter. It is also a "noticia experimental" (*3 Abc.*, 569) — a thing tasted, or known through experience; for this reason, it is called *sabiduría* (from *sapere*).

The intuitive, and completely abstract "image" of Christ is the model after which man must design himself. In speaking of the Ecclesiasticus text — "su costumbre hace diversa la pintura" — Osuna says that some people model themselves on animals, others on devils. However, once knowledge of the Divine is attained through knowledge of the creatures, man can know, and change, himself.

The processes involved in the change are given in the Ecclesiasticus passage. One is intuitive knowledge of Christ, which is "la semejanza de la pintura." (The *semejanza* is our concept; the *pintura* is Christ, the visible manifestation of divine ideas.) If we give our hearts to the concept, we love Him, and we approach Him, since desire is movement through space. "Custom," or habit, changes the picture of the self to conform to the concept or ideal, just as the old customs created the image of lion, serpent, or pig. "El uso que doma a los fieros animales quasi les muda la naturaleza...." [3]

Between seeing the "image" of Christ and conforming to it, however, lies the work of a lifetime. First, the old habits must be broken. This "breakage" — "quebrantamiento" is Osuna's term — is contrition. He says that in this state, the spirit is broken down into dust, which is a perfume agreeable to God (*5 Abc.*, fol. 23). It should be recalled that the Ecclesiasticus text refers not to painting but to the making of seals. "Dust" and "breakage" are more understandable in the context of seals. Also, the seal is an emblem of baptism, where the "ser de gracia" is infused. In the

---

[3] *1 Abc.*, fol. 49. Plato also states plainly this objective of contemplation: the contemplative should, by learning the harmonies and revolutions of the world, "bring the intelligent part, according to its pristine nature, into the likeness of that which intelligence discerns ..." (*Timaeus*, loc. cit., 114).

early church, baptized people were called "illuminated" (*iluminado* is *alumbrado*).[4] Contrition is also called by Osuna "attrition;" both words etymologically had the meaning of "rubbing or wearing away."[5] The figure utilizes the concrete value of words in order to express their abstract value.

Since habits alter nature, the new image of the self is to be imprinted by new customs. [Compare the expression *estar impuesto* (to be accustomed). Osuna uses this locution. (*5 Abc.*, fol. 83)]. These new habits will be spiritual exercises (*1 Abc.*, letra B, tratado 7). The transformation wrought by them will not be finished overnight: "ni la arte ni la naturaleza no pueden transmutar ni convertir unas cosas en otras sin proceder ordenada y limitadamente de una transmutación en otra hasta venir por todas las presupuestas a la última que ha de introducir la forma mejor" (*2 Abc.*, fol. 144).

Therefore, the condition most necessary to any spiritual exercise is its continuation. For this reason, Osuna says, the first three letters of each alphabet always include the words "siempre" or "mucho" (*3 Abc.*, 473). The *tilde*, appended by Osuna after the last alphabetical letter, signifies perseverance. Perseverance is also symbolized by the tail of the animal sacrifice (Leuiti. 3.c) (*1 Abc.*, fol. 52).

Motive power enough to erase the old image and create the new can only be found in the source of all energy, love. "Dará su corazón a la semejanza de la pintura, y velando acabará la obra."[6]

The expansion of language. Conscious as he is of both real and linguistic phenomena, Osuna complains of the limited resources of language. In respect to contemplation of the creatures, he says that it brings to your knowledge many things that cannot be written (*2 Abc.*, fol. 129). One reason they cannot be expressed is that the language ("romance") cannot properly declare spiritual matters, "por la falta de los vocablos que importan conveniencias y relaciones y dispusiciones y maneras de se aver unas cosas con

---

[4] See the Catholic Encyclopedia, XIV, 324-75.
[5] Cassell's *New Latin Dictionary*.
[6] The process may be hastened by the operation of grace. To attain such a grace is the purpose of *recogimiento*. This will be discussed in more detail in Chapters VII and VIII.

otras o entidades y cosas apartadas de la materia corporal y grossera a la qual está nuestro vulgar muy atado." For example, in its "operación e impression espiritual" the eye can perceive "contrary" colors in one place, which it cannot do in its "operación real y exterior" (*2 Abc.*, fols. 90, 91). (I think he refers here to the negative after-image of sight.)

In short, subjective phenomena share some canons with objective ones, but not all. A convenient example can be taken from music, which can figure, in a melodic canon, the activity of reason tracing a cursive pattern of form; in a chord, it can figure a formal pattern perceived as a simultaneous concept. However, the figure itself imposes a canon unsuitable to its spiritual analogue; music in audible. This forces the writer using such a figure to combine a noun like "music" with an incompatible or contradictory attribute; e.g., "la musica callada" (San Juan, *Cántico*).

The figure of "vision," which also represents conceptualization, has the advantage of silencing an importune sense-referent, but it evokes another. Mental concepts are not really seen. Osuna's passage cited from Richard of St. Victor illustrates the difficulty of working with this figure. The writer is forced to say that the intuitive concept is like a picture, but not like it. In our present context, we could say that it is like a picture in presenting a composite of details simultaneously, rather than successively through time, but it is unlike a picture in being invisible, and in being able to present energy (action and potential action), as well as matter. Again, the problem may be solved linguistically by paradox or oxymoron; in the case of the visual sense, it can result in some statement that light is darkness, or vice versa; "la noche es mi alumbramiento en mis deleites," is an example that Osuna uses, borrowing from Scripture (Psal. 138 b) (*3 Abc.*, 366).

A similar difficulty occurs in dealing with space relations as figures of category position; Christ the Eagle is highest in divinity as he is lowest in humility. Many subjective states are ordinarily expressed in terms of space relations — *abatido, exaltado, salir de sí, ensimismado, arrebatado, recogido*. The geometry of such relations in the material world is not quite congruent to that of the spiritual world. Mixing the two results in sets of incompatible statements.

Since the canons of material and spiritual entities do not precisely coincide, the writer is forced to suggest first one set and then another in order to rectify the false suggestions of the one, and to embody the ineffable phenomena of the other. Language itself has selected certain canons of its own, not all of which convey perfectly the objective world (one case is that of fire, the substance of which is inseparable from its attributes), or the subjective one (the highest contemplation is defined as a state of knowledge in which nothing is apprehended that can be spoken). Linguistic canons, however, are useful in their own right. The language permits abstracts to be constructed on the basis of concrete terms; this canon is exploited by Osuna in his use of *conocer, concebir, alumbrar, ver,* and *contrición,* for example. He then exploits the concrete aspects of each term according to their many canons, and attaches these to the abstract or subjective aspect of the word.

Besides furnishing in this way limitless resources for expression, the distinction between concrete and abstract levels is correlated to Osuna's customary division of the universe into "corporal" (accessible to the senses) and "spiritual" (purely subjective) phenomena. It is also related to the distinction between visible and invisible things, which defines the state of contemplation.

The language itself, when it represents both these worlds in one term, is using a "figure" to which we may be so accustomed that we are no longer conscious of its nature. But if the figure is new and unaccustomed, the canons must be painstakingly traced, as though we were defining the words of a new language.

Basic to the definition of a "figure" is the establishment of patterns of operation in the reality it represents. Several quite different entities may hold one or more of these patterns in common; for example, the painting of a picture, the conception of a child, or a clear visual impression of the sun may all represent the formation of a concept in the mind. Since all these activities have a common canon, they themselves can be subsumed under one concept. Contemplation of the creatures consists of formulating just such concepts. These may be called "words" in the sense of "parable-word" as we have discussed it. Such words, I believe, are those that Osuna has in mind when he says that spiritual exercises are the words of God, and that his alphabets are designed to teach the letters of which they are composed.

In our own ordinary language we can point to examples of condensation into one word of two things having only a function-pattern in common. Such concepts are expressed in *concebir* and *conocer*, for example, and in any constructions where physical phenomena represent subjective ones; that is, where we, like Osuna, have used the physical world to represent the spiritual. Cassirer points out that the delineation of concepts, and consequent application of "words," is based on the process of detecting similarities in function, in languages taken generally. For example, if "dancing" and "working" are considered (as among some primitive groups) to fulfill the same function (produce crops), the same word will be applied to both activities. [7]

Our unconscious acceptance of the customary figures of our own language is noted by Proust:

> Au fond, les anciennes formes de langage avaient été autrefois, elles aussi, des images dificiles à suivre, quand l'auditeur ne connaissait pas encore l'univers qu'elles peignaient. Mais depuis longtemps on se figure que c'était l'univers réel; on se repose sur lui. [8]

The technique of classifying by function, for which the language itself provides a model, is employed consciously by Osuna, with the difference that some concepts he evolves may not have a name in Spanish. They can be expressed only in a complex formula like a sentence. Therefore, he charges ordinary words with new canons. One word like "águila" will be used to express a whole set of such formulae. The reader must then manipulate the word, with all its new connotations, together with other words of the same nature. He is forced into the process of evolving a new language, and through it, to look at the world anew as he traces analogies and correspondences previously unseen.

---

[7] Ernst Cassirer, *Language and Myth*, transl. by Susanne K. Langer (New York, 1946), 40.

[8] Marcel Proust, *A la recherche de temps perdu* (Paris, 1954), I, 552.

Chapter V

OSUNA'S DIALECTIC AND RHETORIC

Scripture and the book of creatures. Topics of meditation, according to Osuna, may be scriptural texts or things from the world of nature. Both are taken as matters of fact. Osuna distinguishes, within these categories, four classes, which he calls "books". They are: "el libro de las criaturas," "el libro de fortuna" (human events), "la Escriptura," and "el libro de los buenos" (example set by good people). These "books" (given in ascending order of excellence according to Osuna) "open the eyes of the soul" (*5 Abc.*, fol. 80).[1]

Some of these materials for meditation will be seen, others heard. For example, sermons and lessons contain words that one must keep within the heart, "refiriẽdolas y cotejandolas unas con otras," as Mary treated the words of Christ (Luc. 2.g) (*2 Abc.*, fol. 126). This meditation disposes the soul for the other things it should do, and prepares it for mental prayer. "The breath of good thoughts lifts the wings of desire." This meditation is a ladder on which to rise to God (Jacob's ladder). Its steps are the good words — sermons and lessons — that are meditated. Without

---

[1] Ruth Wallerstein has remarked (*Studies in Seventeenth Century Poetic* [Madison-Milwaukee, 1965] 32), that two principal forces motivated belief in the "book of the creatures" as the "alphabet of God:" the metaphors and parables of the Bible itself, and the doctrine that Old Testament history is a "symbolic prefiguration" of the life of Christ. Both things and words serve as images and parables, according to Tertullian.

Wallerstein attributes the symbolic interpretation of Biblical names, through their etymologies, to the Hebrew tradition specifically. It is important in Philo (39).

this meditation it is impossible to arrive at the perfection of contemplation or at the form of life that the Christian religion demands (*2 Abc.*, fol. 127).

Doctrine that we see includes that offered by the things of nature. This is also an *escalera*; Osuna says that we can, with industry, love God for every one of the created things, "usando della como de escalón para sobir al amor del Señor, holgándonos y agradándonos por haver creado nuestro Señor cada yervecica y dotándola de singular gracia..." (*3 Abc.*, 497). Also "lo corporal fue criado para que ayudase á lo espiritual, en especial á nuestra ánima, que de otra manera no puede comenzar á elevarse á las cosas invisibles de Dios.

"Y no sólo ayudan á los hombres, mas también á los ángeles; los cuales; según Sant Augustín, cuando fueron criados, subieron al conocimiento del Criador contemplando ordenadamente las obras de los seis días. Así que todos subimos é abajamos cada uno en su manera por el escalera [*sic*] que es la orden de las cosas criadas" [*sic*] (*3 Abc.*, 321).

In practice, Osuna shows a certain predilection for the contemplation of nature. Of such meditation, he says that it is laudable and was followed by many saints. The Lord made the creatures for this purpose. Continuing, Osuna says that the meditation of nature is the science, of those that we "humanly" investigate, that brings the most joy. Inspired by his own obvious pleasure in the natural sciences, Osuna includes in his books a quantity of 16th century notions about it.

Osuna says that each person will extract a different doctrine from his meditation, depending on what mental attributes he brings to it. Meditation of the creatures may illuminate the understanding as well as excite love in the soul, and the same logical methods are to be used in meditation that are used in explicating Scripture. Osuna devotes several folios in the letter R of the Second Alphabet to the praise of science, reinforcing his statements by various scriptural citations, including Solomon: "El que ama la buena costūbre ama la sciēcia" (Pro. 12a). Study and contemplation, which are doctrine and prayer, are both necessary to Christian life. They are equivalent, respectively, to listening to God, and speaking to Him. Scriptural figures of these processes are Martha and Mary.

Although Osuna says at first that each individual will extract a different doctrine from his meditations, he does not accept all such conclusions as valid. Instead, he insists on systematic reasoning processes and on the acceptance of dogma.

When speaking of Scripture, Osuna says rather surprisingly that it, too, yields different interpretations, according to its reader. It is like an animal whose fur is no more inclined to lie one way than another, or like those images that seem to look at the viewer wherever he may stand,[2] like a chameleon that wears the color on which it is put, or a mirror that represents whatever stands before it.

However, it is necessary to subject oneself to the rules of the faith. The ancient philosophers erred, at times, for lack of the dogma. Specifically, they turned the "causes of things" to their "carnal" (i.e., material) sense. An example given by Osuna is the statement that primary causes are limited by secondary ones. God, the first cause, cannot be limited. But a philosopher "con solo la lumbre natural" contemplated visible things and came to know invisible ones. [Plato?] According to Osuna this visible word is "sacado y hecho a la traza de aquel mundo ydeal y imitable que es esse mismo dios" (2 *Abc.*, fols. 126-31).

In the Fifth Alphabet also, Osuna recalls the ancient wise men, who through knowledge and speculation, and deducing some things by means of others, pursued God. Such thoughts are "philosophical riches." (5 *Abc.*, fols. 183-84).

The previous chapter showed Osuna's treatment of a creature (the eagle) as a vehicle for meditating the grandeur of Christ. Among other statements of the eagle's activities, there figured a scriptural text that was utilized as one of the canons of the figure. It was interpreted (1) as representing historical events, the Incarnation and Resurrection, and (2) as a figure of redeeming grace conferred on the contemplative through the act of knowing.

These correspond to the allegorical and anagogical levels of Biblical exegesis. In utilizing, as he does, the canons of material things as patterns of spiritual activity, Osuna follows an ancient

---

[2] Nicolas Cusanus compares this type of picture to the eye of God. (Edgar Wind, *Pagan Mysteries in the Renaissance* [New Haven, 1958], 179-80).

tradition, which he has applied not only to scripture but to other data. For example, he extracts a tropological interpretation from the eagle's examination of his offspring: i.e., it is necessary to examine one's thoughts and intentions.

In fact, the practice of Scriptural exegesis and that of meditation do follow the same general principle. It consists of detection of canonicity in various operations performed by material or abstract entities. The literal and metaphoric levels correspond roughly to visible or "sensible" phenomena, the tropological may include both "sensible" and intelligible, and the anagogical is primarily intelligible or ineffable.

Nicolás de Lyra, who is cited by Osuna frequently in the Fifth Alphabet, states the case clearly in other terms: "Littera gesta docet / quid credas allegoria / moralis quid agas / quo tendas anagogia."[3] Osuna himself lists the four levels: *literal, alegórico, moral, anagógico*. As an example, he uses the story of Longinus. On the literal level, he was a cruel man, who, to please the officials, thrust his spear into Christ's side to be sure that He was dead.

Allegorically, Longinus represents Christianity. His lance is Faith. The iron point is Love. The iron "hace camino por Christo muerto," that is, through the death of Christ, it passes to the portals of blessedness.

Anagogically, Longinus is the Christian who wants to be released (*desatado*). [This is release from the flesh, whether in death or in infused contemplation.] The lance is the sigh (*suspiro*) that wounds Christ with a prayer like an arrow. The wound in Christ's side is the abbreviated paradise [into which the contemplative wishes to fly] (*6 Abc.*, fol. 13).

Forms of spiritual exercise or mental prayer show similar correlations: *cogitatio* confines itself principally to the literal sense of words, and *contemplatio* to the purely abstract. To progress from one level to another requires the process of "referring and comparing some things to others" (recommended by Osuna for meditation of Scriptures and of the creatures), which makes

---

[3] Harry Caplan, "The Four Senses of Scriptural Interpretation," *Speculum*, IV (1929), 286.

possible the detection of canonical forms, or correspondences, as they are frequently termed.

In the Second Alphabet, Osuna discusses meditations of Scripture and of the creatures without making any significant distinction between the two, except that the materials of one are heard, and the other, seen. In practice, he interprets Scripture with considerable freedom, although it would be difficult to ascertain how much of this apparent liberty actually has some support in tradition. On one occasion, Osuna cites four authorities — the "glosa ordinaria," Bede, St. Jerome, and Lyra — in their interpretation of the text under consideration. After explaining the suitability of each view, he gives his own version (5 Abc., fol. 100). (He may, however, have based his opinion upon some source that he does not name.)

It would be difficult to account for the similarity in Osuna's treatment of Scripture and of natural history without recourse to the tradition to which he is heir. The methodology of Biblical exegesis, adapted to the extraction of doctrine from history and parable, is applied by Osuna to other types of material. In this, he was continuing a practice that was already venerable. St. Bonaventure, the great Franciscan, supported the proposition that the visible world is a mirror of its Creator, Who can be known through observation and deduction.[4] Osuna attributes to St. Augustine an admonition to meditate the creatures: "Porque no puede ser visto de nosotros en qué manera es Dios bueno en su naturaleza, nos amonesta que lo veamos en sus obras..." (4 Abc., 238). He remarks also that "the philosopher" has called "blessed" those who can know the causes of things (5 Abc., fol. 183).

Caplan[5] attests to the emphasis on the four senses of Scripture in medieval sermonology. Charland remarks that the practice of confirmation by authority was borrowed by preachers from the exegetes, who were the university preachers. The relation between

---

[4] Julius R. Weinberg, *A Short History of Medieval Philosophy* (Princeton, 1964), 165.

[5] Caplan also remarks ("Four Senses," 284-85) that the multiple levels of interpretation passed from Hebrew exegetical tradition into Christianity through Origen, Philo, Augustine, and Jerome, having been sponsored by the school of Alexandrian Neoplatonists who attempted the reconciliation of that philosophy with Christianity.

preaching and sacred hermeneutics was drawn even closer by the preacher's use of concordances. [6] Osuna is both an exegete and a preacher. Some of his sermons can be seen in *Norte*. Gilson comments on the fact that things designated by sacred texts became symbols, which were then subjected to interpretation themselves. [7] It is only a short step from this to the application of the exegetical method to anything from the created world; in short, to treat material from the "books" of the creatures, of fortune, and of good example in the same way that Scripture was treated.

A tendency toward this development may have appeared early. St. Thomas Aquinas remarked:

> The multiplicity of these interpretations of Scripture does not cause ambiguity or any sort of equivocation, since these interpretations are not multiplied because one word signifies several things; but because the things signified by the words can themselves be types of other things. [8]

In this passage Aquinas has clearly pointed out a progression from the Scriptural word to the thing itself, with its characteristics. [9] Since one Scriptural text was used as the basis for an entire sermon (Charland, "Artes," 112-13; Gilson, *Idées*, 101) the introduction of figures served to help extract the full meaning of the passage. Also, this was thought to provide material that would strike the imagination, be retained in the memory, and give pleasure to the hearer — especially an unsophisticated one. Charland cites Thomas Waleys, a Dominican of the fourteenth century, to the effect that such figures are pleasing and are retained in the memory, "étant plus en conformité avec notre mode natural de connaître *per conversionem ad phantasmata*" ("Artes," 205). Gilson cites the anonymous Franciscan author of the *Ars concionandi* to the same effect (*Idées*, 113, 131, 142). This Franciscan,

---

[6] Th.-M. Charland, "Artes Praedicandi: Contribution à l'histoire de la rhétorique au moyen age," *Publications de l'Institut d'Etudes Médiévales*, VII (Paris and Ottawa, 1936), 166.

[7] Etienne Gilson, *Les Idées et les lettres* (Paris, 1942), 147.

[8] *Summa Theologica*, I, art 10, Reply Obj. 3: cited by Caplan, "Four Senses," 287.

[9] I am not entirely convinced that all ambiguity is averted. However, the important item here is St. Thomas' recognition of the possibility of further development through the creature, used as a type.

like Osuna, compares the world to a book: "modum istum dilatandi si quis exercere vult, librum utilem habet, scilicet mundum, cujus omnes partes instruent ipsum et trasmittent and Deum. Uti poteris mundo tanquam figura ..." (*Ars concionandi*, III, 44, cited by Gilson, *Idées*, n. 1). Such use is observed by Gilson in the practice of the popular preacher Michel Menot. Exposition of the theme by means of such figures is one of the traditional eight modes in use through the medieval period (Charland, "Artes," 204, 211).

The Dominican Thomas Waleys and the anonymous Franciscan of the *Ars concionandi* both point out the necessity of knowing the properties of creatures in order to utilize them in exposition (Charland, "Artes," 204; Gilson, *Idées*, 141-42). Waleys, who considers figures the most fecund mode of exposition, says that the work of preparation consists of isolating the "conditions" of the thing to adapt it to the subject of the sermon. The conditions consist of its intrinsic attributes (essence and accidents, quality, quantity, operation) and the extrinsic ones (causes, final and efficient; effects; other accidents — place, time, etc.). Charland identifies the list, which is not completely given, as the ten categories of Aristotle ("Artes", 205).

Osuna, in his instructions for contemplation of "virtues, or any other thing" gives as one method the "diez predicamentos" — considering the thing according to (1) its substance, (2) its quantity, (3) its quality, (4) its "relation," (5) its passion, (6) its operation, (7) its situation, (8) the place, (9) the time, (10) its "habit." Concluding his chapter on methods of contemplation, he says: "Digo te de verdad q̃ te es tan necessaria forma y orden en tu meditaciõ, como las partes en la rethorica porque no menos ha de ser adornada la rethoria [*sic*] divina que la humana" (2 *Abc.*, fol. 133).

Osuna's "predicamentos" are Aristotle's ten categories, designed to elicit an exhaustive description of an entity. (These are the "predicables," many of which are determined by what can be attributed to a thing by means of the copulative verb.) [10] One point

---

[10] Charland, "Artes," 53. Definition of some of the categories is still a matter of discussion; for a brief account see "Categoría," *Encyclopedia Universal Ilustrada*, Espasa-Calpe, S. A., XII, 529-30.

that bears on our subject, however, is the fact that the types of attribution considered here are not confined to static qualities; they include functions and relations. For example, in living things the categories "quantity, quality, place" may elicit the attributes of growth, change, and independent movement (G. M. LeBlond, *Logique*, 351-52). In fact, LeBlond points out that Aristotle conceived of form in terms of function; he expressly denies (in *The Parts of Animals*) that it consists of external configuration or color. An example given is the difference between the sculptured hand and the living one: only the living one can perform the functions that define a hand. This concept of form and function is basic to Aristotle's idea of the soul (*Logique*, 358-59).

Another method of meditating the creature that Osuna recommends is to consider the thing within itself according to its virtues and nature, its generation, its "active or passive corruption," its mixture or the composition of its parts, or "en orden a otra cosa" (2 *Abc.*, fols. 132-33). This system seems to derive from the first; it is a more detailed set of categories of things that a subject may do, or that may be done to it, and ends with a suggestion to consider the subject's relation to something else.

These processes throw considerable light on Osuna's method of arriving at the canons of his figures. In practice, the elements he chooses as significant are usually functions and relations. In describing an entity he may follow the course of dialectic rather than rhetoric, and the attributes elicited by these methods determine the meaning of the thing named. Since these categories are designed to bring forth all possible attributions to a subject, their usefulness in Biblical exegesis is obvious: through some canon of the things, an obscure passage could successfully be explained.

The medieval preacher found figurative texts to be fruitful themes, because of this potential for expansion (Charland, "Artes", 205). This was important, since the preacher was restricted to one text as the basis for his entire sermon. Possibilities of developing a theme through the use of figures are practically infinite. Every concrete entity, and especially a living one, has enough attributes, and relations with other things, to make possible a progression from figure to figure. For example, in explaining the eagle, its attribute of eyesight led to a development of the figure of "vision." Through the word *alumbrar* this figure was linked to that of birth. All these figures were necessary to a complete explication of the brief scriptural text, which also introduced the words "monte" and "mercader," two figures having a number of attributes of their own.

Basically, development of a theme through figures depends on discovery of similarities in canons. Coincidences in words are also exploited, as shown by several examples in the last chapter. There, we also saw the use of an etymological meaning to establish the connection between an abstract word and a concrete figure — "contrition," the "wearing away" or "breaking up" of the figure on the seal.

This, too, is an established device of Biblical exegesis, and of medieval preaching technique. An example of the possibilities inherent in etymology may be shown by Osuna's treatment of Biblical names (sacred onomastics). He says, for example, that "Jacob" means "luchador," and that he represents Chastity (*4 Abc.*, 681). His other name is Israel, "poderoso con Dios." Now, he is a figure of the Christian peoples (*1 Abc.*, fol. 45). However, he is also a figure of Christ. The two names signify the divine and human natures (*4 Abc.*, 570).

Again, "Jacob" may be translated as "acoceador," and "Israel" as "hombre que ve a Dios." In this lengthy explication Jacob is the good bishop, who undertakes a hard task to win a wife (the church). He becomes a pilgrim. First he must take Lía, "la muy trabajosa" — that is, a difficult post, and not the one he wants.

Jacob is "acoceador" because he has subjugated his vices (they are "acoceados y sojuzgados"). As Israel, he sees God with the eyes of the mind — intellect and will.

The pasture of love for the will is found in interior affections (*recogimiento*). Pasture for the intellect is found in doctrine. The good bishop is obliged to supply his flock with both.

Jacob said to his father-in-law: "Mientras moré contigo no fueron estériles tus ovejas, ni comí los carneros de tu ganado, ni te mostré pieza que bestia fiera hubiese comido, y todo el daño te pagaba, porque lo hurtado me demandabas" [Gen. 31: 38, 39].

The sheep are parishoners who grow in virtue. They are given salt (discreet words). (Elisha threw salt into the waters of Jericho so that the fields would bear fruit.) The bishop eats the sheep when he occupies his best people in his personal business affairs. To "leave the flock in the desert and go to watch the fight" is to go to Paris to debate.

Eating the sheep may also represent nepotism, or signify misappropriating funds intended for charity. The wild beasts may be (1) the bishop's officers, or (2) error, or partisanship (of opinion), or (3) vices and bad habits.

However, God demands an accounting of the souls of the parishoners. Christ is the true Shepherd; no one can be a good *pastor* without transforming himself, by love, into Christ (*4 Abc.*, 663-67).

In this example of text explication, Osuna begins by identifying Jacob as the "good bishop," but the principal base of the similarity (the pastoral occupation) does not immediately follow. Rather, a secondary resemblance (the first marriage) is introduced. This is followed by an explanation of the significance of the names. Between these two "declarations" there is a difference of "level" — "acoceador" is interpreted tropologically, through words with strong material associations. "He who sees God" has, naturally, an anagogical meaning. This leads to the first suggestion of sheepherding — the "pasture" (*pasto*) used in its figurative sense. This effects the transition to the scriptural text:

"Mientras moré contigo no fueron estériles tus ovejas, ni comí los carneros de tu ganado, ni te mostré pieza que bestia fiera hubiese comido, y todo el daño te pagaba, porque lo hurtado me demandabas."

In "declaring" the text, the first figure is explained, and is followed, not by the second one (*carneros*) but by an item, salt, drawn from outside the passage. This is not only interpreted but reinforced by allusion to another text, Elisha sweetening the waters (IV R. 2d). The declaration of figures then proceeds. But another new element is introduced. This intrusion shows an incongruity of "tone," and is inserted for critical pungency and comic value — "to leave the flock in the desert and go to watch the fight."

The figures continue: the wild beasts are the officials of the diocese. This figure strikes the attention, partly because it is a one-to-one equation of one living material being with another. This is not the case in any other figure here, except the sheep (who are really "souls"). The concrete image is, in fact, effective, as the medieval theorists held (Charland, "Artes", 133-34). However, abstract interpretations are later introduced.

The final line, "todo el daño te pagaba, porque lo hurtado me demandabas," is given on its literal level — an accounting is demanded, the loss is paid. Coming after a long series of transpositions to the tropological, the literal words have gained, by contrast, the force of reality. The threat is genuine, not metaphorical.

Another change of level is immediately introduced: to be a good *pastor* one must transform oneself by love into Christ. Here, the play on *pastor* (shepherd or lover) ties the two threads of discourse together. Also, the anagogical level, left incomplete after "the eyes of the soul," is again picked up. The reader is tempted to fill it in completely. However, this level is introduced for another purpose besides that of suggesting a new canon. It offers to the hearer an immediate course of action designed to avoid fulfillment of the threat. In short, it meets the rhetorician's or the preacher's demand that the hearer be persuaded to some frame of mind or course of action.

Osuna's treatment of this passage shows two of the principal techniques of theme development practiced in the medieval sermon (Charland, "Artes", 200-206). These methods — development through words (etymologies, double meanings, etc.) or through figures — are mixed, in order to keep the audience interested, as well as to derive the full weight of doctrine from a brief Scriptural passage. The technique of beginning with a point that does not immediately reveal its connection to the main theme is also advocated by the medieval theorists (Charland, "Artes", 146-47). The method piques the interest of the hearers, who are left wondering what is to become of the first thread of discourse.

Insertion of authorities (Biblical texts or others) was demanded by preaching practice on the grounds that the sermon should never go long without support from accepted doctrine (*Charland*, "Artes", 166). An advantage that accrues from the insertion of new texts is the opportunity to embark on a new chain of words and figures. Had it suited Osuna's purpose, he could have declared the text of Elisha and the salt, a theme offering many possibilities. It is not unusual for Osuna to undertake the development of two themes, and to reconcile them successfully.

It was not considered good preaching practice to present an argument in undisguised form (*Charland*, "Artes", 147). If we extract the argument from Osuna's *dilatatio*, it goes as follows: The good bishop, through wise counsels and administration, protects his flock from sin and error, and makes its members increase in virtue. To be such a bishop, it is necessary to conquer one's own vices, and to have a good conception of what virtue is. If you undertake the mission and do it badly, through negligence or corruption, you will be punished. In order to avoid this, you must study doctrine and practice *recogimiento*, which will teach you how to improve.

One of the noticeable contrasts between this summary and Osuna's work is a transposition of order; the theme of study and mental prayer is mentioned before the motive for its practice. Otherwise, however, after the text is enunciated, the succession of topics is logical.

The material before the text stands in the place of the introduction to the theme in the sermon. Coming before the text, it often consisted of a series of affirmations confirmed by the text itself. In Osuna's hands, the order of elements is curious: first, the extraneous similarity between the bishop and Jacob; then the text and the declaration of each name, from which develops the word-play that connects the introduction with the theme. Such organization is designed to create confusion and suspense, which will later result in a feeling of satisfaction as disparate elements are resolved.

The advantage of the figured style lies, in great part, in its demand on the attention of the audience or reader. As a result of increased attention and the effort of following such an exposition, the concept, once complete, seems new.[11] This advantage, when the preacher is limited to traditional subject matter, is incalculable.

---

[11] Some psychologists affirm that belief itself may be defined in terms of attention. If the mind is filled by an idea, "with its congruous associates," it consents to the idea. William James, *Psychology*, 1890, 564; cited by William E. Utterback, "A Psychological View of Argumentation," in *Studies in Rhetoric and Public Speaking in Honor of James A. Winans* (New York, 1962), 286. The first condition necessary for an idea to prevail in the mind is that it bring with it a considerable emotional intensity (*Ibid.*, 287).

One of Osuna's systems for meditation is in effect a concise plan for a portion of a sermon, the declaration and development of the theme, and the peroration. He says that the method may be applied to "virtues or anything whatever." "From afar," he says, contemplate (1) the excellence of the virtue,[12] (2) its degrees, (3) its definition, (4) a special reason to praise it, (5) an authority, (6) an example, (7) a figure, (8) how evil is its contrary, (9) why the thing is virtuous and deserves to be loved, or why it is commanded of you, or counseled you, (10) why it is suitable to you because of your office, or for your utility, or for your necessity. And, finally, consider why you are deciding to seek the virtue, the means of seeking it, and the end for which you do it (2 *Abc.*, fol. 133).

This type of exposition seems particularly suited to the contemplation of abstracts (for example, love — of God, of neighbor, of self). It reveals a rather orderly scheme of encomium, distinction, definition, appeal to authority, example, illustration, definition by the contrary, and peroration. Although Osuna may change the order of these elements, they all form an important part of his stylistic resources. He may turn them to humorous ends, incidentally: the meaning of "Beati pauperes spiritu" is clarified by its contrary "maledicti pauperes sine spiritu" (5 *Abc.*, fol. 191).

A fourth method of contemplation given by Osuna refers specifically to creatures, and shows a decidedly Franciscan attitude. First, contemplate God in each creature. Then consider that the creature is given to you, and that you are its neighbor and close to it. Then divide the first consideration into three parts: (1) how God created the creature, conserves it and concurs in it; (2) how He redeems it; (3) how He honors it, giving it an "office" or goodness or grace or "spiritual virtue."

Next, contemplate the creature in relation to yourself as an individual: first, as an example of how to live; second, its use to the corporal man; third, how you enjoy all the goods of the

---

[12] I believe he means to contemplate the virtue in its general sense. This would be consistent with his instructions on contemplating the field, and also with preaching practice in declaration of the theme. A term to be explicated was taken, when possible, as a totality, so as to permit further distinctions and subdivisions (Charland, "Artes," 167).

creature as if they were yours, and should therefore sympathize with it, and favor it (*2 Abc.*, fol. 132).

Obviously, the preparation of books or sermons by techniques such as those described in this chapter required a considerable supply of source material. For scriptural interpretation, various glosses were available. Osuna cites "la glosa interlinearia y la ordinaria que es de Sant Augustin," (*5 Abc.*, fol. 107 *et passim*) and the gloss of Nicolás de Lyra (*5 Abc.*, fols. 106, 109 *et passim*). On Biblical translation specifically, he refers to Theophilato (*5 Abc.*, fol. 194), and the Septuagint (*5 Abc.*, fols. 109, 122, *et passim*). Some of the other sources that are mentioned in the Fifth and Sixth Alphabets with documentation sufficient to indicate that they were probably used directly are: St. Jerome, St. Chrysostom, St. Ambrose, St. Augustine, Duns Scotus, Mombaer (*Rosetum*), Pliny (*Natural History*), Pedro de Ravena, and the letters of Hernando del Pulgar. The Fifth Alphabet suggests, by its general tone, its inclusion of texts in Latin, and its comparatively careful documentation, that it is directed primarily to the clergy. Osuna is careful, however, to address himself specifically to the lay reader at some points.

Osuna cites many authorities, in addition to those above. How many he consulted directly, and how many through secondary collections, would be difficult to determine.

For his data on the creatures, Osuna sometimes refers to Pliny or Aristotle. Beyond these, he seldom divulges the source of his scientific notions or of his exempla. The latter are rather sparingly used. However, Osuna does include incidents from his own life, which he uses as exempla, and which supply some facts of biographical interest.

Osuna's data, in its turn, apparently became source material for preachers. De Ros mentions a letter (1532) from Matthias Weynsen, a *comisario general* of the Franciscans, approving Osuna's Latin sermons, and reporting that his vernacular books were used as sources of doctrine by the preachers of Spain.[13]

---

[13] De Ros, *Maître*, 608. This probably helps to explain the numerous editions of the works in the sixteenth and seventeenth centuries. Of those in Castilian, the First Alphabet went through six editions; the Second, five; the Third, six (before 1639); the Fourth, six; the Fifth, three; the Sixth,

Gilson remarks on the mutual relationship and influences of sermons and doctrinal works (*Idées*, 153-54); in Osuna's case, both are produced by the same author, and their structural similarities are clearly to be seen.

Emotions. Osuna's aims are those that St. Augustine designated for the preacher: *docere, delectare, flectere*.[14] In order to teach and to persuade, the appeal to emotion is invaluable, and Osuna loses no opportunity to stir the reader by a horrifyingly realistic description of the Passion (*1 Abc.*, letters E and F), by exhortation, exclamation, reiteration, direct discourse, and especially by the use of concrete figures and comparisons. Moreover, he instructs the reader on the role he should play. The Alphabets are spiritual exercises and the reader's part in them is not passive.

In the introduction that precedes the First Alphabet (it actually introduces Alphabets One through Three), Osuna invites the reader: "Ven como familiar amigo, ven con ánimo enseñable, y de hecho serás enseñado...."

He continues: "Hormiga prudente se puede llamar el devoto que con llaneza de corazón va leyendo poco a poco llevando intento de hallar alguna palabra que le mueva su afición a Nuestro Señor; y desque la halla detiénese allí llamando las vecinas potencias de su ánima y sus deseos para que se gocen con la pieza de oro...) (*1 Abc.*, fol. 6).

In short, the reader must be disposed to learn and to welcome any incentive to holy love that he may find. Osuna predicts that his reader will prefer some parts of the Alphabets to others; he

---

two. The *Gracioso Combite*, before its suppression by the Inquisition, appeared in six editions, and the *Norte de los Estados*, three or four. The most popular Latin work, *Pars Occidentalis* (a collection of sermons), went through nine editions, and was published in Antwerp, Paris, and Lyons as well as in Spain (Zaragoza and Medina del Campo). The next most popular Latin work, *Pars meridionalis*, appeared in seven editions in Spain, Paris, Venice, and Rome. During this same period translations appeared; the "Passio Compassionis" (a sermon from *Pars Occidentalis*) was translated into Italian (1573); the First Alphabet and the *Gracioso Combite* were translated into Italian (1583 and 1599, Venice), the Sixth Alphabet into Latin (Rome, 1616), and the Fifth into German (2 editions; 1602 and 1603, Munich). De Ros, *Maître*, 167-73.

[14] See Joseph A. Mazzeo, *Renaissance and Seventeenth-Century Studies* (New York, and London, 1964), 12. Mazzeo points out that St. Augustine's source is Cicero.

says that you like "one member of the Lamb better than another," but that He, like manna, tastes like each person's favorite dish. However, to have fervor, you must believe that you have it, and do violence to yourself in order to seize the kingdom of heaven. You must force your thoughts to enter "the narrow door" — the wound in Christ's side (*1 Abc.*, fol. 52). The narrow door leads into Christ's heart, the mind of the Logos (v. Chapter VII).

Osuna says that during the first year of practice, mental prayer (spiritual exercises) does not usually yield any feeling of devotion. One must persevere, until he seems to see with his eyes what he thinks in his heart, and until his affections correspond to his thoughts in such a way that tears will come immediately upon thinking of something sad (*3 Abc.*, 466).

It is so important to cultivate sensitivity to the mental image that Osuna refers to it frequently. One simple spiritual exercise is to carry in the imagination at all times the image of Christ, or of the Cross. Looking at this image often imprints it more into the heart. Much practice makes it easier to retain. Habit permits you to be moved even by the slightest reference. If you see a figure of Christ (a material one such as a painting) that seems to inspire you with devotion, you should retain it in your memory (*2 Abc.*, fols. 41, 42).

By practicing, says Osuna, you learn to induce affections in the heart whenever you want to feel devotion. You must be able to do this quickly. At first you will think that you are doing nothing. The spirit, however, is mobile and stable — if it is quick to good works it is firm in virtue. You must feel at various times joy, fear, wonder, love — these changes give you control of the heart, and soften it.

> Ca no deves pensar cosa sin la embestir en tu corazón para que assí la sientas y representes en ti mismo con buenas mudanzas de la diestra del muy alto: porque assí como el cantor según los puntos muda la voz: assí el que ora ha de hazer en sí mismo diversos sentimientos formando en el corazón lo que piensa y desta manera representará los mysterios como en farsa más por obra que por palabra (*2 Abc.*, fol. 50).

The term "farsa" has, for Osuna, a broad sense of dramatic representation. The Mass is a "farsa" in which Christ Himself comes to represent His own actions (*Convite*, fol. 28). Osuna's emphasis on actions and operations as revelation of spiritual reality, along with the importance of imagery to arouse emotions, may indicate to us some of the rationale for the developing religious drama.

Meditation is superior to reading, according to Osuna. He cites David: "Entendí más que los que me enseñavan: porque tus testimonios eran meditación mía" (Psal. 118) (*1 Abc.*, fol. 21). Contemplation, says Osuna, requires complete concentration. Like a painter who is happy while painting a happy picture, the contemplative almost transforms himself into what he is doing; but in interior operations, the degree of concentration and of transformation are both greater (*3 Abc.*, 482).

In this new reference to the art of painting, Osuna refers again to the transformative influence of the mental concept. The purpose of this "softening of the heart," and of intense concentration on a concept, is the changing of the form on the seal, or the "reformation" of the soul, modeled upon the new concept.[15]

Prolixity and abbreviation. In the second prologue to the First Alphabet Osuna says that he had prepared some brief and easy grains of doctrine, the *letras*, which his friends had passed from hand to hand. Since some were glossed by other people in a way he did not approve, he was obliged to declare them himself. Each *letra* is an *espiga*, and includes "lirios y flores con que se cerquen nuestro trigo, que serán razones e figuras y profecías para mayor hermosura y fortaleza de nuestro dezir: porque según Sant Hieronymo la verdad tanto es más señora y más fuerte quanto es más vestida de razones que justas le vengan."

Ships cannot move without extending their sails, nor birds fly without spreading their wings. In the present case, "es mejor la maldad del varón que es algo prolixo, que no la mujer que haze bien en ser breve ..." (a reminiscence, perhaps, of Juan Ruiz). In this book (the First Alphabet) the doctrine appears in abbreviated form at beginning and end; in the middle "se dilata para que mejor se imprima en tu corazón siendo por más razones confirmada" (*1 Abc.*, fols. 5-6).

---

[15] In the context of this theory, it is not difficult to see how Don Quijote transformed himself into a knight-errant.

Later, Osuna again describes the structure of the Alphabets, and cites the authority of precedent. He says that people who write of important things have the custom of stating briefly the substance of the matter at the beginning. Then they treat the subject "quasi en confuso" with long declarations. This method was used by "el filósofo en las doctrinas morales,"[16] and by David in Psalm CXVIII, where the substance of the matter to be taught is put briefly, "y después dilata los medios para la alcanzar." Thus, Osuna continues, he puts in the first *letra* of each Alphabet a brief rendering of the subject that will be treated prolixly in the following letters. He asks the reader to look at the letter A in Alphabets One, Two, and Three. From each word of the distich of the letter can be drawn "una buena sentencia." By way of example, Osuna explains the principal words of his letter A of the First Alphabet (*1 Abc.*, fols. 9-10). This process is carried to a further extreme in the following treatise, in which the distich reads "Bienauenturado es el que de sus fructos [los de la Pasión] goza." Each chapter included in the treatise begins with one of the ten different letters of "bianauenturado," and each discusses a different "fructo" (*1 Abc.*, fols. 14-22).

Osuna's treatment of the "letra" in his Alphabets is similar to the preacher's treatment of his theme, or sometimes, of his introduction to it. (If the distich serves as introduction, then a scriptural passage is introduced as the theme.) From the distich (or the Scripture), the body of the treatise is developed by methods of *dilatatio* based on those of the medieval sermon, with heavy reliance on the use of figures and the declaration of words. When alphabetical organization is lacking, the same techniques of development are applied to Scriptural texts or statements by the author or by authorities.

One of Osuna's stated reasons for the use of the alphabetical form is its potential as a memory aid (*1 Abc.*, fol. 4). Each distich, I believe, is supposed to recall to the mind of the meditator the contents of its corresponding treatise. The relationship of the distich to its treatise would often seem tenuous or arbitrary if it were not referred to the traditional methods of sermon composition.

---

[16] As far as I can discover, Aristotle's *Ethics* is not organized alphabetically, but his *Metaphysics* is.

Osuna treats his own words in the *letra* in the same way that he treats a scriptural text. He interprets them on various levels (tropological and anagogical, frequently), and subjects them to distinction, definition, subdivision, and development by means of figures, word declarations, and examples, and confirms them by authority.

In order to develop a whole treatise from a few brief words, the words must be chosen with care. Often they represent large categories that may embrace many sub-classes or elicit long descriptions and discussions. Osuna says that the first letter in Alphabets One, Two, and Three enunciate the theme of each book. These letters show the very general nature that the distich may have. In the treatise on the Passion (The First Alphabet) letter A reads: "Anda mucho escodriñando la passiõ y causas della" (*1 Abc.*, fol. 6). Here, *anda, pasión*, and *causas* offer material enough for many different meditations.

In the Second Alphabet, letter A is "Amor se deue mezclar entre todas las potencias" (*2 Abc.*, fol. 16). It begins with the attributes and types of love, and proceeds to extract from *amor* and *todas las potencias* a series of treatises on spiritual exercises of every type and for every occasion.

The Third Alphabet begins with "Anden siempre juntamente la persona y spíritu" (*3 Abc.*, 323). The book deals with the formulation of a concept of Christ (by means of *recogimiento*), and the translation of this spiritual reality into action.

By his procedures of development, Osuna derives a great deal of material from a brief theme. The abbreviated form is easily remembered. It is developed as though it were a theme for a sermon, by dialectical or rethorical methods. As a result, Osuna's words become invested with a great weight of meaning. He says of scriptural words that they represent many things, because they resemble Christ "quien, siendo una palabra que una vez habló Dios, contiene en sí todas las cosas." The Gospel "figures" many mysteries in one (*4 Abc.*, 485-86). The same statement may be applied to Osuna's own words, which he glosses as extensively as Scripture, and by the same methods.

Obscurity. Words so charged with meaning are likely to be cryptic to the uninitiated. Osuna's remarks on meditating Scripture could apply equally well to his own works. For extracting hidden meaning, he offers some practical advice. Osuna says that apparent contradictions or anomalies in Scripture are an indication that spiritual meaning should be sought (*5 Abc.*, fols. 35, 36). Also, the figure that represents many things may not perfectly fit all of them, because it cannot accommodate all the particular attributes of each (*2 Abc.*, fol. 107).

Searching out the interior meaning is a laudable exercise. According to Osuna, mysteries and figures are used so that the righteous will acquire merit, and will exert themselves in ruminating and thinking about "lo que les es dicho no a la clara." You must seek the treasure of wisdom as one seeks hidden wealth (*2 Abc.*, fol. 107).

In respect to his meditation on the Passion, Osuna applies these general statements more precisely. He says that other books on the topic in *romance* treat the Passion of Chirst as though it were that of some other martyr. He intends to "subir algo más en estos mysterios para que los afilados ingenios de algunas personas devotas tengan en que emplear muy fructuosamente sus pensamientos. ... Estos mysterios más delgados no se deven esconder pues que Christo los publicó ..." (*1 Abc.*, fol. 3).

From the actual content of the First Abecedario, one way of "rising higher" into the mysteries seems to consist of applying to Christ the Man what is said of God (this is named as one method of contemplating the grandeur of Christ) (*1 Abc.*, fol. 104). But since divinity cannot be spoken of directly, it must be spoken of by comparison with some other thing. Under the "earth" of Christ's humanity must be found the gold of divinity. "La humanidad se ha con la divinidad como se ha la figura con lo figurado" (*1 Abc.*, fol. 99).

In Treatise XV of the First Alphabet the cosmic nature of the Word is set forth. "Esta luz que es dios luze en las tinieblas e las tinieblas no la comprehendieron" (Joa. 3.c). The shadows may be the creatures; in them God shines "algo oscuramente," but they do not show all His attributes and perfections. In this sense they do not "comprehend" Him. One method of contemplating the divine grandeur is to divide it up among finite creatures, such as the eagle, tree, or star. Also, the light in shadows may be Christ in the world, or Christ in the prophecies and figures of the Old Law, which cover the Divine (*1 Abc.*, fols. 103-104).

To discover the divine Christ, the anagogical sense must be extracted from the human life of Christ, from the Scripture, or from the creatures. Another source of revelation is the Sacraments. They all, according to Osuna, represent the Passion, which is the source of their virtue. Also, anything contemplated as a representation of the Passion comes to be a sacrament (*2 Abc.*, fol. 134). In contemplation, apparently, anything in the world may be spiritualized or sanctified.

Since it is a meritorious exercise to discover the anagogical meaning in all things, Osuna provides an opportunity for the "refined wits" of some devout persons to do so. He may stimulate the process by supplying a few elements of the anagogical in a predominantly tropological development, as was the case in the declaration of Jacob-Israel. A reader familiar with the canons of the figures and attuned to word-plays can fill in the missing pieces of the anagogical interpretation, using as guides those elements of it that Osuna does include. In Osuna's prose, apparent anomalies are often indications that we should seek a spiritual meaning, as he counseled us to do with Scripture. This process is meditation or contemplation, depending on the materials manipulated.

In this way, Osuna composes passages that mean one thing to the beginner, and several things to the contemplative who is able to compose his own counterpoint over the *canto llano* of the literal meaning. A rather ambitious example of this type of composition is offered by Treatise IV of the Third Alphabet. Since some of the anomalies that indicate the presence of an unstated anagogical meaning are found in the context surrounding the treatise, it will be necessary to describe briefly this portion of the Alphabet before we consider the treatise itself.

Chapter VI

MEDITATION OF A FIGURED PASSAGE:
ITS CONTEXT, ITS CONTENTS,
AND A SCIENTIFIC PROBLEM

The First Three Alphabets. As their titles indicate, the *Abecedarios* all bear at least a tenuous relation to one another. Within the set there is reason to believe that the first three were planned as parts of one composition. The prologue published with the First Alphabet is an introduction not only to the First, but also the Second and Third. According to this prologue, the parts represent three phases of Christian doctrine. They are compared to "pan de centeno, pan de cebada, y pan de trigo" (*1 Abc.*, fol. 4). The Third, or "pan de trigo," can be expected to be the most substantial and to refer to the divine Christ, Who is the Wheat that, in dying, produces fruit [Jn. 12:24]. The grain of wheat, to Osuna, is the heart of Jesus (*6 Abc.*, fol. 4). In the Third Alphabet, the word "pan" is identified with "deleite" (*3 Abc.*, 462). "Our daily bread" is sometimes Christ the Son (*3 Abc.*, 463) and sometimes the delectation enjoyed in contemplation (*3 Abc.*, 458, 507). Wheat and bread, have, of course, many symbolic associations. The host is made of wheat, Osuna says, because it was so in the offerings of the Old Law (*Convite*, fol. 15). In the Old Law, the Host is prefigured in many instances, among them in the barley bread, cooked beneath ashes, that descended on the armies of Madian. This bread represented the sword of Gideon who conquered the Madianites [Jue. 7:13, 14]. The ashes are the *accidentes* (attributes) of the bread itself; the Word of God is the "espada del espíritu que como en vaina se esconde en la hostia" (*Convite*, fol. 45).

The Word is both doctrine (spirit), and matter. "Verbum charo factum est, et habitavit in nobis" is glossed by Osuna, who says that as if He really dwelt *within* us, he animates our souls. As the host, He enters into us and gives back to us flesh — which is what He took from us — just as the host becomes flesh upon the altar. This bread does not cease to be doctrine (*verbum*) (*5 Abc.*, fol. 115). The Divine Word that appeared in visible form (in Christ) became invisible again under the aspect of bread (*Convite*, fol. 75). This bread is wheat to those in the active life, manna to contemplatives. It is "living doctrine" because it is always true (*5 Abc.*, fol. 16).

The magic numeral three has been associated with many natural triads; among them is that of beginning, middle and end. As has been noted in Chapter II, the delight of contemplation, which can be figured in the wheaten bread, is a provisional end. It is the repose of will in the desired object, and in this sense it is the "end" — attainment. However, this union is by nature transitory, and to make it permanent the entire trajectory of life must be changed, so as to achieve permanent possession in Heaven. The provisional "end" therefore becomes a new beginning.

In the Third Alphabet, as many pages are devoted to the exercise of Christian virtues as to the matter of contemplation itself. This is entirely appropriate, since the objective of all spiritual exercises is the determination of how to act. Moses ascended the mountain of contemplation, but what he brought back were the tablets of the Law. The Third Alphabet, therefore, contains both manna for contemplatives, and practical moral guidance. The first two *Abecedarios*, covering as they do the meditation of the Passion and other spiritual exercises and disciplines, lead to the summit of contemplation and to moral reform, which is the subject of the Third.

Within this last text, I have chosen for analysis the fourth treatise, because it shows how tropological and anagogical levels may be constructed over a highly figured passage, using the methods of contemplation suggested by Osuna. Many of the figures are explained, at least in part, in previous portions of the

Alphabet. Others are not glossed by Osuna until later, if at all. Probably the meaning of the figures in Treatise IV will not come to light until the whole series of three Alphabets has been read, and perhaps read more than once.

In this chapter, I shall first place the fourth treatise in its context. In the following chapters, I shall give a synopsis of it, and shall try to supply the pertinent canons of the figures. In the process, the treatise will gain new dimensions, and its enlarged meaning will be summarized.

The position of Treatise IV. In the organization of a serially numbered *Abecedario* few anomalies of order should be expected. Nevertheless, at least one occurs in this work: Osuna remarks in Treatise V that the fifth treatise occupies the third place (366). (All page references in this Chapter, unless otherwise noted, refer to *3 Abc.*). Since a careful study of the first five treatises reveals nothing out of logical, numerical, or alphabetical order, one might postulate that Osuna has begun counting with Treatise III, where, for the first time, information about the practice of *recogimiento* is actually given. The prologue and the first two treatises include some explanations and glosses, but they really compose a lengthy and varied exordium. They could both be summarized as an admonition to practice *recogimiento,* and to give thanks to God for this promise of Glory, and for the sample of it that is found in infused contemplation. This brings up the alternative possibility that the triad in question may be *exordium, narratio* and *conclusio.* Or possibly it is the three acts named by Ficino: God "primo singulo creat, secundo rapit, tertio perficit." (*Rapere* is used to signify the divine seizure.) (Wind, *Mysteries,* 48 and n. 1). Since Treatise IV, which is in the second place, deals with this rapture, and Treatise V with moral reform, this triad is a possibility. Less likely here, I think, is the series discussed by Martz in *The Poetry of Meditation*: [1] one-composition (setting the scene, the work of memory); two-analysis (work of understanding); three-colloquy (work of the will). These refer to meditation, not contemplation in the sense that we have defined it here.

---

[1] Louis Martz, *The Poetry of Meditation, A Study in English Religious Literature* (New York and London, 1966), 38.

Another possible triad is formed by the three hierarchical acts: purgation, illumination, perfection (*3 Abc.*, 467). Of this series, the first two appear in Treatise IV itself.

With the third treatise (perhaps the first in the triad), actual instruction in the theory and practice of *recogimiento* begins. The letter reads: "Ciego y sordo y mudo deves ser y manso siempre." Reference is made to the same letter in the Second Alphabet, where the eyes, ears, and mouth are identified as the "three doors" to the heart — a concept that is important to the interpretation of our treatise in the Third Alphabet. Although the admonition of letter C in the two alphabets is identical, the glosses are not the same; they are, rather, complementary. Both *Abecedarios* demand in letter C the discipline of the senses. In the Second, this is developed principally from the tropological standpoint (don't listen to flatterers, don't speak ill of others). In the Third Alphabet, mortification of the senses consists of their complete extinction in *recogimiento*.

The reason for suppressing the corporal senses, in the Third Alphabet, is to see better, and to know better, by means of interior vision. Our intellect, in divine things, is like an owl or a bat; it has so little light in its eyes that it cannot look on the sun's light. Efforts to comprehend the sum of God's works becomes overwhelming, because of the disproportion between His greatness and our understanding. Those who scrutinize the majesty of God are dazzled by its magnificence, since sensible things, if excessive, "corrupt" the sense. Similarly, although the intellect is incorruptible, great revelations may disturb it, "overturn" it, or make it temporarily cease to function. Out souls are like *mosquitos* that burn themselves flying toward the light.

The foregoing references to sense and intellect are, by extension, allusions to the imagination and to the rational function, and to the sensible and intelligible worlds. Both of these are inadequate to the task of knowing the Divine. Not only that; they must be consciously suppressed before experiential knowledge can be attained.

The solution, when all else fails, is to banish all thoughts of any kind whatever, converting all the forces of the soul into a fervent desire, guided by "una noticia que no se refiere a criatura alguna" (353). Thus Moses entered the cloud on the mountaintop before speaking to God. To inspect or speculate on the grace of divine communication is to lose it. It can only be felt, and that only when all other vital operations have ceased. For this reason God says: "No me verá hombre y vivirá" [Ex. 33:20] (350).

Grace is necessary to the achievement of pure contemplation. Although the capacity for knowing (*conocer*) God exists in the soul in principle, it is impeded by our preoccupation with human things. It is like a seed or plant, whose generative power cannot act without sunlight, or like an egg "movido y avivado con el calor de la paloma" (the Holy Spirit). But we cannot, in any case, understand (*entender*) the essence of God while we are in this life, and people should be careful to speak with discretion of spiritual things. The letter C advises that we be blind, deaf, and dumb, not only physically, but mentally. The intellect must entertain no thought, the will no love for created things, and the memory must not propose anything that can be spoken — that is, anything from the sensible or intelligible worlds.

There remains the admonition to be meek, or to be willing to conform to the will of God. Since the ecstatic state is a flight of the soul, comparable to death, the contemplative must be absolutely resolved to follow the will of God wherever it may take him. The meek are compared to glass vessels (*vasos*) protected by straw; they are humble and patient and solicitous of guarding, with the bond of peace, their unity of spirit.

This ends the third treatise, and the fourth begins: "Desembaraza el corazón y vacía todo lo creado." Since we already know that sight, hearing and the word are three doors to the heart, this letter appears, at first glance, to be a repetition of C. In the course of the text, it does seem to develop further many of the same ideas, though in more figurative language.

After the encomium of the meek, the fourth treatise starts with an introduction in the form of a *praeteritio*. This "letra," says Osuna, is *not* addressed to the mundane, the hard of heart, or those with divided interests. A whole chapter is devoted to reprehending such conditions, in spite of the fact that after Osuna has showered blessings upon the meek, we might expect this treatise, with its title, to reflect another Beatitude: "Bienaventurados los que tiene puro su corazón, porque ellos verán a Dios" [Mt. 5:8].

Then, after a long encomium of the scriptural text "Guarda tu corazón con toda guarda, porque dél procede la vida" (Prov. IVc), the heart is compared to a series of figures that will be seen in the next section. Before we examine these, however, we should look briefly at the contents of Treatise V, so that the environment of Treatise IV will be clearly established.

In Treatise V, the discussion now turns on good works, and on the effects of *recogimiento*. Here, too, we find the statement by Osuna that this treatise occupies the third position. He has just previously noted that everything has a beginning, middle, and end (or "yerva, espiga y grano"), so we can be reasonably sure that the third position is the end. Knowing as we do that good works are the "end" of contemplation, we can see that Osuna has chosen an appropriate subject for the conclusion of this series. The first member of this series, Treatise III, discussed the principles of contemplation; what is still lacking is a treatment of the state itself. This ought to find its place in Treatise IV, the contents of which appear in the following summary.

A summary of treatise four: "Desembaraza el corazon y vacía todo lo criado." Osuna begins his gloss of this letter with a crushing denunciation of the mundane man. It is a complete change of rhetorical pace, following, as it does, the eulogy of meekness. It is a *sforzando* in the composition. Osuna says:

> Esta nuesta letra, pues habla del corazón, cosa clara es que no será dirigida ni se dirá á los que no tienen corazón. No se dice á los descorazonados que no tienen resabio ninguno de espíritu en sí; mas biven como si no tuviesen corazón ni ánima, á los cuales dice Dios (Hie. XVIIb): Maldito sea el hombre que confía en el hombre y pone su fortaleza en la carne y su corazón se aparta de Dios, porque aquéste sera así como retama en el desierto, y no verá cuando viniere el bien; mas morará en el desierto en sequedad, en tierra salada y que no se puede habitar (355).

This plant represents the man who is solicitous only of the flesh, and who is cursed as follows:

Id, malditos del mi Padre, pues ninguna misericordia tuvistes conmigo, sólo con vuestra carne, confiando en el hombre exterior que de fuera parece y olvidando el espíritu interior que es invisible (355).

Such misguided people will surely end up in Hell. The *retama* (desert broom) is fit only for burning, being useless, fruitless, and bitter. It lives in the desert, isolated from God's help, and without one tear of devotion to water it. The earth is salty, which provokes thirst even more.

Such a heart is never satisfied, because material things cannot quench its desire. They only increase it, as salt increases thirst. This is because the heart of man is made in the triangular shape of the Trinity, and Vices, being round, cannot fill it. (Vices are known to be round because they go rolling down to Hell.)[2]

This treatise is not addressed to the heartless, nor to those with two hearts; i.e., divided interests. "En las cosas que se impiden unas a otras, la pérdida es riqueza." An example of this is the second set of teeth coming in before the first set has come out. Another example is the case of a man with two heads. A friar with worldly interests is like the two-headed man. He is also "el pecador que entra á la tierra por dos caminos" (Ecli. IIc); "él que hace mal y espera bien."

The hard of heart are also excluded; they are worse than the rock in the desert, because they will yield no tears even when struck by the blows of fear and of love. Some hearts are hard as diamonds.

Neither is this treatise directed to those that have not tamed their hearts. They have hearts like unhooded hawks carried in

---

[2] This allusion may be to Osuna's rather obscure "declaration" of a text from Psalm 82: "In circuitu impii ambulant." Osuna compares the condemned soul to a stone that, shot from a sling, goes through the air with a spinning motion. According to Osuna, the Judge throws the stone down to Hell, saying at the same time "Ite, maledicti ..." (5 *Abc.*, fol. 46). These are the same words that begin Osuna's curse. There is reason to suspect a concealed meaning in Osuna's introduction of "roundness" as the unique cause for man's dissatisfaction with worldly things, especially since the circle and sphere usually have celestial connotations. Osuna says that things that move in a straight line move themselves; those that move in a circle are impelled by the will of God, as are the heavens (2 *Abc.*, fol. 132).

the hand. The hawk will fly at anything it sees. It must be blindfolded and let to fly only at the divine prey.

If our hearts are not uplifted to spiritual things, it is not because God has failed us, but because we have failed Him. We must put our hearts upon our shoulder, like the good shepherd who finds the lost sheep and carries it home. (The shoulders are "grandes deseos é altos ejercicios.") This spiritual exercise — *recogimiento* — consists of "hacerle [al corazón] una jaula de perpetuo silencio." ("Ninguna cosa hay más huidora que el corazón.") At this point the principal text is stated: "Guarda tu corazón con toda guarda, porque dél procede la vida."

The second chapter consists principally of a long encomium of this text, in which "is resolved the entire law of God." The words should be graven in the heart, the seat of life.

Next there comes a brief statement of the heart's function, which will be discussed in detail in the following section.

In Chapter III of this treatise appears the first of the figures representing the heart. It is the castle. (This figure is now well known because of its appearance in the work of Sta. Teresa.) There are three ways in which this castle may be taken or damaged; by deceit, by force (fear), or hunger (evil desire). These correspond to the three lances Joab sank into the heart of Absalom, and they are the motives of Adam's fall, and Judas' condemnation.

Against these three dangers are arrayed three powers of the soul: reason, irascibility, and will. (The usual listing is intellect, memory and will. The change is significant; we should recall that, in Chapter II, irascibility is identified as an aspect of will. Besides its defensive function mentioned in Treatise IV, it is the power that seeks the useful.) In this treatise, Osuna compares irascibility to the sword: "cada uno tenía su espada sobre el muslo por los temores nocturnos" (Cant. IIIc). The thigh connotes chastity, which is to be rigorously guarded.

Osuna also makes an implied comparison between the irascible power and the spoken word. He relates an anecdote about the martyred St. Vincent, who reprimanded another Christian for responding meekly to the judge that was trying to frighten them. According to Osuna, St. Vincent said. "¿Por qué estás hablando entre dientes y con palabras mansas á aqueste sobervio?

No cures sino con exclamación, para que con la mesma autoridad de la voz su ravia, que ladra contra su señor, sea quebrantada."

Apparently, there are times to be meek, and times to be irate. "Buena ira" is defined by Osuna as zeal for justice. He cites St. Thomas (*Convite*, fol. 61).

Against the attack of evil desire is ranged the appetite for celestial things, the aspect of the will that seeks what is pleasing.

The heart is now compared to the terrestrial paradise, which must be guarded by the cherub and the flaming sword, "ligero de bolver." The terrestrial paradise is the country-house of God (*casa del campo, casa de deporte*) and is, in fact, the heart. It is the "casa del campo del rey Salomón;" "huerto del rey Asuero." Grace is the fountain that irrigates this paradise; it divides itself into four principal streams, the cardinal virtues.

There are three kinds of trees in this paradise. The forbidden tree — knowledge of good and evil — represents the individual will. Of this tree we must not eat; we must do what is commanded and avoid what is prohibited.

The tree of life is spiritual wisdom and "gusto sabroso de la contemplación." Other trees are virtues; their fruits are good works.

This paradise is guarded by the cherub (knowledge of spiritual things), who defends it against error. The cherubim in Ezechiel's vision raised their wings and flew, so that the wheels would be raised above the earth. The wheels are our hearts, which must lift themselves above mundane things.

The flame (of the flaming sword) is divine love, which destroys the things of this world, as Sampson's foxes destroyed the crops. This love drives away the flies (worldly temptations) like hot steam from a boiling kettle. Fire has the property of separating different things and uniting like ones. This flame defends the door of the will.

The third door of the heart is sensuality. This is defended by the knife (sword); fear of God. The knife "circuncidará a todas las demasías de la carne."

Another figure of the heart is the Ark of the Covenant. The three items it contains (the tablets of the Law, manna, and the rod) correspond to the cherub, flame, and sword.

Again, Osuna reiterates the importance of guarding the heart, from which all life proceeds. The snake, whose life comes from its head, uses its whole body to protect the source of life. Similarly, the roots of the tree are protected underground.

The heart is susceptible to damage from all sides. It is like the bilge of the ship [3] that collects everything that comes aboard. For this reason all sense impressions and experiences must be carefully controlled.

The heart is more movable than mercury, and more subtle; it escapes and goes where least expected.

The fifth and last chapter of the treatise is on the application of this *letra* to *recogimiento*, which is the most important part of all. Here, the maxim means to vacate the heart of all created things, leaving God alone in it. When a great king comes to visit a private house, it is customary to remove all the furniture; the king has his own brought in.

Thoughts that "tremble" (i.e., change) are shaky hands (¿*manos de azogado?*) holding a vessel that can never be filled, because it constantly spills over. When the senses are stilled, and there is no thought of created things, God proceeds from the heart in silence, like the waters of Shiloh. His *minero* is the heart of man. He is Life; and from the heart "proceeds Life." His mission is to animate the soul and unite it to Him, as the human *ánima* flowing from the heart gives life to the body and unites it to the soul.

The emptiness of the heart in *recogimiento* is represented by the widow's empty vessels that Elisha miraculously filled with oil (IV Kings IV). The woman is a figure of spiritual wisdom — "el gusto dulce de las cosas celestiales." The vessel, if presented empty of all created things, will be filled completely with grace.

---

[3] Osuna uses the word *bomba,* but defines it as follows: "La bomba del navío es un lugar que está en medio dél, al cual se acoge toda la agua que en el navío se derrama, y también cuando el navío está abierto por alguna parte y por allí entra agua, todo va á parar á la bomba, por estar en medio de la nao y más baja que todas las otras partes della" (363). This must certainly be the bilge. *Bomba* is used in the sense of *sentina* in another instance also (*5 Abc.*, fol. 70); there I see no reason to suspect any hidden purpose in his use of the word. Nevertheless, I have not yet found *bomba* used in this sense in a dictionary or in any other writer; its normal meaning is "pump."

The Virgin at the moment of the Annunciation is the most perfect example of *recogimiento*.

Recogimiento is like the chaos that preceded creation. Before the Holy Spirit came upon the waters, the earth was empty and vacant [*sic*]. As a symbol of this, God commanded that a hollow altar be made for Him (Ex. XXXIX) of light and incorruptible wood. The sacrifice on this altar (the heart) is our "buen deseo." As Saint Paul said (I Cor. XIIId), we leave the things of children for those of manhood, and similarly we must leave the contemplation of the creatures for that of their Creator. Jeremiah says, "Levántate, loa en la noche, en el principio de las vigilias: derrama así como agua tu corazón delante el acatamiento del Señor" (Jer. IIa). We must lift our hearts from created things to un-created things, and praise the Lord in the night that is the deprivation of sense. Then we can say (Ps. CXXXVIIIb): "La noche es mi alumbramiento en mis deleites."

We must pour out of the vessels (our hearts) all human thoughts. This "derramamiento" is not like that of the broken vessels (non-recollected hearts mentioned in Treatise I). Rather, it is an evacuation caused by great heat from the fire of love.

The conclusion of the treatise consists of what is actually a list of figures applied to the heart. Osuna does not attempt to explain them. They are as follows:

> lámpara de la virgen prudente; la ración del noble gavilán que con sólo el corazón se satisface;[4] consistorio divino donde Dios trata sus secretos; fornaz donde el ángel de gran consejo viene a refrigerar los que en El andan; cámara del verdadero Heliseo; vaso de oro lleno de maná de gracia en el arca del pecho; incensario; pesebre del niño Jesus; cama florida de El; arco de la amistad de Dios, puesto en las nubes de las lagrimas; ciudad pequeña de Dios; libro de la vida; santo sepulcro del cuerpo de Cristo; brasero de oro del templo.

The heart is all these things, provided that is empty, as it should be, and guarded by all possible means.

---

[4] God "eats only hearts;" that is, He evaluates not the work, but the desire that inspired it (2 *Abc.*, fol. 195).

As a trained logician and rhetorician, Osuna cannot fail to recognize that his conclusion, which ought to be either the logical result of proof or the fulfillment of the reader's expectations,[5] is neither. The argument of the fourth treatise is a *petitio principii*; it says that we should guard our hearts because they are castles, arks, etc., and that if we do guard them they will be a similar set of items. Remembering, however, that this is the middle treatise of a set of three, it could be the "espiga" of the triad "yerva, espiga y grano." A wheat-head contains many grains, which probably correspond, in this case, to the numerous figures. In these figures we should look for a *narratio* appropriate to the context of this portion of the Third Alphabet. In this investigation we shall "declare" the figures, to see if they yield this *narratio* on another level.

In order to discover the analogies between the heart and the figures representing it, it will be advisable first to investigate Osuna's views on that organ itself. It has already become apparent that he ascribes to it some role in intellectual activity. By gathering together his statements about the heart, many of the qualities that he attributes to it will come to light.

The heart and the blood. In the heart is found the *ánima*, or sensitive soul (384). This is reflected in its triangular shape, a figure of the Trinity. The angles are identified with the three powers of the soul: memory, intellect, and will (356). It follows that Osuna can say of the heart that it includes all the life and operations of man (2 *Abc.*, fol. 10).[6] It also follows that the heart contains the principle of good and evil. Every external movement proceeds from a "primer movimiento" that takes place in the heart. Thought is the root of action; the fruit is good or bad, according to the root (359).[7] As the site of will and intellect, the heart is the source of thought.

---

[5] For the requirements of a conclusion under the laws of dialectic or rhetoric, see C. S. Baldwin, *Medieval Rhetoric and Poetic* (New York, 1928), 222.

[6] My edition of this *Abecedario* is faulty; folio ten should have been numbered nine. I show the folio number given in the text.

[7] Other parts of this tree are named in the Second Alphabet, fols. 87-88. The branches are desires, the leaves are words, the flowers are joys, and the fruit is works. It is also easy to imagine the circulatory system as a tree, the branches being the blood vessels. The first half of the 16th

It is also a repository, for it contains memory. In folio 42 of the Second Alphabet, Osuna says that if you have once formed a mental image it leaves an impression on the heart and remains in the memory. It is easy to see, now, how the heart can be compared to the bilge of a ship, where all seepage is collected; bad impressions will remain there as well as good. Sight, hearing and speech are called the three principal doors to the heart, because we ordinarily think about what we see or hear, and deliver our thoughts orally (2 *Abc.*, fol. 21).

Since the heart is the "seat" of soul, it is appropriate that it is the first organ of the body to be formed by nature, and the last to die (4 *Abc.*, 376). As such, it is the root of all mental activity and the consequent actions, and reformation of the heart results in a total change in behavior (415).

The treatise under discussion depends, for its structure, on the concept that the heart contains the soul, that is, all basic functions of intellect, memory, and will. For this reason, the figures representing the heart will also represent the soul, and we can apply to the heart our information about the soul. This not only clarifies the tenors of the figures; it also reveals that the structure of this treatise is more careful than it appears to be on first examination.

The soul and the body: further details on the heart. The heart has four chambers that correspond to the passions: *gozo, tristeza, esperanza, temor.* (The passions are functions of the will; they were discussed in Chapter I.) If the force of the passions is applied to love, they will be like four wheels of the fiery chariot that lifted Elijah above the earth (4 *Abc.*, 443-44). This comparison explains partially the figure of the wheel in treatise four, where it is identified, however, with Ezechiel's wheel. The passions correspond to the winds from the four cardinal points; for this reason, perhaps, they are represented within a circle (the rim of the wheel); the horizon appears to be round. A text from Ecclesiasticus (33:5) supports the figure: "The heart of a fool is like the wheel of a cart, and his thoughts are like the rolling axletree."

---

century saw a rather wide distribution of anatomical drawings (Singer, *Anatomy*, 97-98).

Anima, resident in the heart and afflicted with these passions, is under the influence of the body. Osuna says:

> Las ánimas, según dice el Filósofo, siguen los cuerpos, porque obran según hallan dispuestas las potencias y órganos corporales, y también siguen el movimiento de la caridad, que es instrumento del Espíritu Santo ... (*4 Abc.*, 399-400) [8]

On the other hand, the higher part of the soul, *espíritu,* "que se rige por la razón sin dar lugar a cosa contraria," is once (325) given as analogous to *pensamiento*; in another place (329) it is comparable to *conciencia*. In view of the first definition, "conscience" seems the more likely equivalent; thought is not always ruled by reason.

In the Fourth Alphabet (540), the body "with its earthly appetites and carnal desires" is called "el hombre de fuera ... el hombre terreno que plasmó y hizo Dios." *Espíritu* is "el hombre de dentro," or "el espiráculo de vida que [Dios] sopló en su cara."

In this passage, carnal appetites and desires, though really immaterial and a part of *ánima,* are classified with the body, or "earth," while the spirit alone merits classification as air, the most subtle substance. Since it is not Osuna's custom to obscure thus the boundaries between the tangible, and the intangible, some further explanation must be sought in the figures of *ánima* and *espíritu* that we discover in his work. This problem is related to Osuna's physiology of the heart and the blood.

Osuna is careful to say that the soul is not really divided into two parts, but that it is spoken of in this way because of its twofold operation; that of contemplating spiritual things, and that of coping with terrestrial ones. He cites St. Augustine to this effect (*1 Abc.*, fol. 134).

---

[8] Charland quotes from a medieval sermon: "Quod est in herbis aut in arboribus humor, hoc est in hominibus amor. Sicut enim ex humore herbae et arbores crescunt, sic homines per amorem incipiunt et augentur" (based on Chrysostomus, *Super Matthaeum,* homelia 19a) (Charland, "Artes," 146). A man who hasn't really a rational life may be compared to a tree (Seneca). (Charland, "Artes," 140-41.) Perhaps such ideas account for the use of the shrub to represent the mundane person.

If *ánima* and *espíritu* are an undivided entity, and one is found in the heart, the other must also be there. Osuna has, in fact, said as much when he said that the heart included all the life and operations of man. This statement could hardly refer to anything less than the total soul; *ánima* and *espíritu*.

Similarly, Osuna says that "el ánima y vida de toda carne esta en la sangre" (*1 Abc.*, fol. 124). Here the term *vida* may refer specifically to *espíritu*, "el espiráculo de vida." The basic meaning of the Latin word *spiritus* is breath, breathing; it is extended sometimes to mean the breath of life.[9]

It seems necessary to infer from the previous statements that Osuna believes both parts of the soul are found in the heart and in the blood. This seems to imply a connection between the heart and the blood, a connection that is fortified by his statement that life proceeds from the heart. In this context, his use of the term "*bomba*" for the heart suggests a theory that the heart pumps blood. As far as is known, western science did not advance a circulation theory until the time of Miguel Servet in 1553. (The first publication date of the Third Alphabet is 1527). Harvey's discovery was published in 1628. An Arab, Ibn An-Nafis, had proposed a theory of pulmonary circulation in the thirteenth century.[10]

The heart was known to be a container of blood, however, in the science of Osuna's day and even in very early times. Galen, for example, thought that blood flowed from the right ventricle to the left through the septum, a view that was generally accepted until the time of Harvey (Singer, *Anatomy*, 177). Galen compared the venous system to a tree having its "roots" in the liver or the abdominal viscera; the root of the arterial system he held to be the pulmonary artery. To him, the heart was only a way-station for the blood and "spirit" (Singer, *Anatomy*, 57-58).

In his treatise, Osuna compares the heart to the root of a tree; it sounds as though he may have had Galen's terminology in mind, and have intended expressly to contest his theory. Osuna has said

---

[9] *Cassell's New Latin Dictionary* (New York: Funk and Wagnalls Co., 1960) s.v. *Spiritus*.
[10] A. C. Crombie, *Augustine to Galileo: the History of Science A.D. 400-1650* (Cambridge: Harvard University Press, 1953), 331.

unequivocally that the heart is the seat of soul, the soul is in the blood, and the heart is the root of the soul's "tree."[11] We need only to read "*bomba*" as "pump" to have most of the elements necessary to a theory of circulation. The remaining factors Osuna could have found in the science available to him, for they had actually been proposed long before. However, Osuna carefully defines "bomba" as "bilge."

Although this topic is peripheral to a literary paper, its connection to the figures of treatise four and its general interest may warrant a brief survey of circulatory theories and Osuna's apparent relation to them.

Some theories about the heart and the blood. Osuna, in speaking of the heart, cites Aristotle on an important point: the heart as the source of intellectual life. (In Ecclesiastes 17: 6,7 the heart is also named as the seat of understanding and thought.) Since intellect is a function of soul, Osuna's version of the Aristotelian view is that the heart is the source of soul. Aristotle thought that the arteries carried both *pneuma* (air, spirit) and blood (Singer, *Anatomy*, 20). His medieval interpreters held that the heart pumped *spiritus* to the brain.[12] Since Osuna has already located spirit in the blood, it appears that he need only endorse this principle, and he will have the heart pumping blood to the brain. If so, we should find in his idea of the brain some relation to the "intellectuality" of the spirit that is brought there from the heart.

Osuna describes the brain as the site of "sentido común, imaginación, fantasía, estimativa y memoria corporal" (*3 Abc.*, 399) (the last he distinguishes from *memoria intelectiva*). "Sentido común" is the "common sensory," the reporting center for the five senses,[13] at least some of which are, to Osuna, "doors" to the heart. Mental images, as Osuna has already said, come to rest in the heart, though we can see that they must originate in the brain. Memory, ap-

---

[11] The tree may also represent the body. *3 Abc.*, 436. There is a possibility, too, that Osuna may recall *Timaeus,* 114, in which Plato calls the brain the root of the soul, saying that is is fixed in heaven, not earth. Man is a plant whose roots are in Heaven.

[12] Lynn Thorndike, *A History of Magic and Experimental Science* (New York, 1923-1941), II, 298.

[13] A. A. Crombie, "Early Concepts of the Senses and the Mind," *Scientific American*, X, No. 5 (May 1964), 109.

parently, is divided between the heart and the brain, having its "corporal" or sensory aspect in the latter spot.

The heart and the brain seem to have a complimentary set of functions — the brain being more sensual, the heart more intellectual. The functions of both are those of *ánima* and *espíritu*, those different, though undivided, aspects of soul. The soul must in some way go from the heart to the brain, and in some way the sensory images formed in the brain must be carried to the heart. We have seen that the Aristotelians held that the heart pumped spirit to the brain; I have not discovered how they accounted for its return. The Galenists, however, thought that the brain elaborated from the "vital spirit" brought in the blood an "animal spirit" that was distributed through the nerves, thought to be hollow (Singer, *Anatomy*, 60).

The Galenic view of the brain as a factory of animal spirit would not be inconsistent with Osuna's presentation of the sensory-*cum*-intellectual nature of the brain. However, he differs from Galen on several points. One is his unequivocal statement that *ánima* and "life" are in the blood; if they at some time separate, he does not say so. Another conflicting point is his naming of the heart as the center of the whole system (*ánima, espíritu, sangre*). Galen had treated the venous system as the carrier of "natural spirit" derived from the liver and intestines; the arterial system as a separate set of vessels carrying "vital spirit" to the brain, where "animal spirit" was made and distributed through the nerves. The heart was considered a chamber in which a small amount of blood passed from the originating (venous) system into the arterial system, being mixed in the left ventricle with air brought in by the trachea and pulmonary vein (Singer, *Anatomy*, 58-60).

Galen's theory, the generally accepted one, shows three kinds of "spirit" having different points of origin. Osuna's insistence that there are only two aspects of soul, and that they are both substantially the same thing, is a radical step toward simplification of the Galenic view, and one necessary to a circulation theory. Osuna also places the source of the soul in the heart, and he says that both forms of it are in the blood. This implies a view that the venous and arterial systems spring from the same origin. For a theory of circulation, he now needs only the idea of the heart as a pump, and a set of vessels to mediate between arteries and veins.

Osuna is familiar with the principle of the pump; he states it in the Fourth Alphabet (403); so if he means to call the heart a pump, there can be no doubt that he knows what such a machine does.

Osuna might have derived a "pumping" idea from the Aristotelians; he did not, however, take his theory of the soul from that source.[14] He cites St. Augustine; and he is peculiarly insistent that the two parts of the soul are not really divided. I have not discovered the origin of this idea. Erasistratus (Singer, *Anatomy*, 25) showed two types of spirit, as did Ficino.[15]

The theory of two types of soul is supported by Scripture (I Ts. II 23): "vuestro espíritu entero, con alma y cuerpo...." There is also scriptural support for the notion that animal life is in the blood (see Lv. 17:11 and Dt. 12:23: in the latter, the blood of animals is to the flesh as the soul is to the body).

Osuna says, citing Leviticus: "El ánima e vida de toda carne está en la sangre." His interpretation of this is so literal that he says that our moral lives conform to the blood we drink; therefore it is prohibited to drink the blood of animals. The obvious converse is that we *should* partake of the blood of Christ, the sacramental wine. (*1 Abc.*, fol. 124). Jean Baruzi comments that in the Hebrew tradition, blood is the seat of the life principle.[16]

Soul and "life" are in the blood; both proceed from the heart (*3 Abc.*, 365).

Erasistratus held that the heart was the source of both arteries and veins, and that it pumped both blood and spirit. He thought that the arteries conveyed spirit and the veins, blood. Osuna seems to agree with the first statements and to disagree with the last; when he says that the soul is in the blood he conforms, instead, to Empedocles.

---

[14] Aristotle believed there were three types of spirit (Singer, *Anatomy*, 25).

[15] Erwin Panofsky, *Studies in Iconology: Humanistic Themes in the Art of the Renaissance* (New York, Evanston and London, 1916), 136.

[16] Jean Baruzi, *Création religieuse et pensée contemplative* (Paris, 1951), 56-58.

Erasistratus knew that the valves of the heart prevented return of the blood or spirit through the same channels, and he had discovered that the capillaries formed an intercommunication system between veins and arteries. The principal obstacle to Erasistratus' discovering the blood's circulation was his idea that the arterial system contained spirit, not blood (Singer, *Anatomy*, 33).

Since Osuna has placed the soul in the blood, he seems to have avoided this obstacle, while retaining Erasistratus' idea that the heart was the center of the whole system. It was through a reversion to the ideas of Erasistratus (among them that of only two types of soul) that Servet developed his theory of the pulmonary circulation (Singer, *Anatomy*, 140).

Osuna compared the function of the heart to the priest's work in the mystical body of the church: he distributes the virtues of the soul (*ánima*) among all the members. He cites Scotus (*Convite*, fol. 87).

He discusses the pulse as follows:

> La virtud del corazón que es el amor en el pulso de los brazos se conoce, y este pulso movedor de la sangre no es otra cosa espiritualmente hablando sino obra y trabajo, porque el amor no sabe estar ocioso ... (*Norte*, fol. 72).

Since we have seen, in Chapter II, the circular nature of love, it is tempting to draw an analogy here, and to say that Osuna has implied a theory of circulation.

As we have seen, all the elements necessary to circulatory theory were available to Osuna. Whether or not he had developed such an idea is still impossible for me to say, but it does appear that he had eliminated some of the principal obstacles that traditional physiology had placed in its path.

Osuna's interest in the heart probably stems from his obvious general concern for the nature of the physical world, and from his role as a promoter of the developing devotion to the Sacred Heart (de Ros, *Maître*, 307-08).

CHAPTER VII

SOME MAJOR FIGURES OF TREATISE IV

Mutability of the heart. Although the question of Osuna's physiological theories has been in part a digression, it yields some information directly bearing on the figures of treatise four. In view of the two-fold nature of the soul, the two-headed man, or the man with two hearts, becomes not just a figure of the friar with worldly interests, but a representation of the human soul itself. One head, or heart, is *ánima*, the sensual nature; the other is *espíritu*. Ficino, who viewed the soul as having two parts, had compared it to Janus (Wind, *Mysteries*, 165 and n. 6).

Osuna also compares the penitent to Janus. He looks back upon the sterile years, and irrigates them with tears. His second head looks toward the future, alert to avoid similar evils (*4 Abc.*, 636). He thus becomes a symbol of the *vía purgativa*, which consists of contrition for past sins and resistance against present and future ones (*5 Abc.*, fols. 165-66). The wheel with four faces, compared by Osuna to the soul with four passions, refers also to the relation between *ánima* and the body. We have seen that Osuna says "las ánimas siguen los cuerpos." Through the passions, *ánima* is influenced by the humors, which in their turn are produced by the four elements composing the body. Osuna says:

> Rueda se llama el corazón por el poco sosiego que tiene bolviéndose y estando cuasi siempre en continua mutabilidad; y esta rueda, que es el corazón, se dice aparecer sobre la tierra, porque sobre el cielo otra cosa será. Y esta rueda tiene cuatro haces, que son las cuatro pasiones é movimientos principales que tenemos dicho, los cuales se

llaman faces porque según el que reina en el corazón se demuda é muestra el rostro.¹ (*3 Abc.*, 328).

The wheel is said to be near the animals (Ezech. 1:1-22) because we share these passions with the brutes, and it is necessary to "tame" them so that the heart will no longer be divided among them. The gift of grace mitigates their power and reinforces the cardinal virtues that struggle against the Passions, to bring peace finally between soul and body.

Since the passions are the four winds, the "cuatro haces" may refer to the four parts of the earth, "el haz de la tierra," and the circular rim to "totality."

If the passions are applied to love (see Chapter II) they become like the four wheels of Elijah's chariot; they lift the soul from the earth. Osuna has said that *ánima* is moved both by the body and by love, the instrument of the Holy Spirit. Osuna compares the will to the *primum mobile*, which moves other spheres beneath it. It moves the "sensitive soul" and makes it conform to reason (*2 Abc.*, fol. 8).

Since love is a product of will, the heart, because it houses the will, can be called the fount of love (*4 Abc.*, 385). Love "reigns" in the blood also (*4 Abc.*, 669). Appropriately, Osuna considers love to be generative — he says that Christ generated a new human lineage with His blood (*1 Abc.*, fols. 120, 124); the birth was from His heart (*1 Abc.*, fol. 31).

If the control of the earthly body, composed of the four elements, is broken, *ánima* is freed to follow the movement of love. Since love has the attributes of fire, it may act upon the other elements themselves, uniting likes and separating unlikes, as Osuna says in this treatise.

Osuna speaks of this transmutation worked by love as a vaporization of solids or liquids (incense and steam in this treatise) or as the melting of a solid (the melting of metals is a figure in the Fourth Alphabet (355): metal or glass occur in the numerous

---

¹ The word *faz* suggests not only *facies* (shape, appearance, face) but also *fax* (a torch, firebrand, light, flame [Casell]. St. Peter [2 P. 3:10] says that with the second coming, "los elementos, con el ardor del fuego, se disolverán, y la tierra, y las obras que hay en ella, serán abrasadas." With Osuna's ideas of the fire of love, this may be what happens to the elements with the Coming that takes place in contemplation.

instances of the furnace figure). Since air is already identified with spirit, and fire as the transmuting agent, this accounts for the four elements in the body's composition. Both liquids and solids can be changed into more volatile substances by fire; in the case of vaporization, the substance is actually "lifted from the earth." [2]

A case in point is mercury, which Osuna compares here to the heart in its mutability. He has remarked earlier in the Third Alphabet (325) that mercury sublimes ("se va en humo"). It is therefore a mineral that changes its form to "air." Since mercury was thought to be a liqued form of silver (Read, *Alchemist*, 92), it seemed to span the solid, liquid and gaseous states. Not unnaturally, it was thought to contain within itself the element of fire. [3] Since it has all these characteristics, Osuna could well choose to compare mercury to the heart, in which *ánima* is related to earth, spirit to vapor and love to fire.

I do not believe that Osuna intends to equate *ánima* with the flesh, or the solid state; he says that it is "influenced" by it. Since the degree of spirituality corresponds in every case to the degree of volatility, or to lower specific gravity, in Osuna's universe, the most suitable location for *ánima* is in the liquid state. Waters, because of their specific gravity, go downward like solids; in this sense Osuna can say rather literally that "las ánimas siguen los cuerpos." In one instance he specifically equates water to sensuality, the distinctive trait of *ánima*. He says that it is inclined downward. Fire is light from the face of God, and is the sinderesis which naturally rises (2 *Abc.*, fol. 156). Water and other fluids may be vaporized by the action of fire; this would correspond to the "spiritualization" of *ánima* under the influence of love. This would make of the heart (a solid container of liquid and "air") a perfect analog to the three states of mercury. It would also account for Osuna's introduction of the figure of steam rising from

---

[2] The alchemists viewed any vapor as "air," any liquid as "water". The terms refer to the "gaseous state," the "liquid state," etc., rather than to specific instances of such states. See John Read, *The Alchemist in Life, Literature and Art* (London, 1947), 5-6. Compare Plato's statement that fire, air, etc., are names of qualities, not substances (*Timaeus*, 48-49).

[3] C. G. Jung, "Transformation Symbolism in the Mass," in *Pagan and Christian Mysteries: Papers from the Eranos Yearbooks*; ed. by Joseph Campbell (New York and Evanston, 2d ed., 1963), 109.

the boiling kettle, and the injunction to "Pour out your soul like water...." (The figure of the kettle will be discussed further on.) Moreover, Jung points to an ancient tradition ("Transformation," 108) equating soul to water. Osuna, in this treatise itself, compares the soul in *recogimiento* to the chaos before the Holy Spirit came upon the waters.

Blood and mercury are both "waters" in which fire dominates; they manifest the same "principles." One of their attributes is mutability, the capacity for change. This principle is symbolized by the snake and by the flaming sword (Jung, "Transformation," 110-112). The prototype of both these "waters" is the blood and water that flowed from Christ's side; it was known to the alchemists as the "fiery form of the true water," "spiritualis sanguis," and similar names (Jung, "Transformation," 109). This blood and water is the water of baptism, according to Osuna (343). The analogy is probably seen in the "spiritualizing" or "life-giving" operations of the three substances.

The snake, a relatively inconspicuous figure in Treatise IV, assumes unexpected importance in conjunction with mercury, the flaming sword, and the word, for all of these may represent the Logos (Jung, "Transformation," 110-11). Like so many of the figures in this treatise, the snake is used by Osuna to represent at least two divergent ideas.

In Treatise IV, the snake is a figure of prudence; he coils himself about his head to protect the center of his life, a model of the way our hearts should be guarded. Since the snake with his tail in his mouth is a symbol of mercury, this figure of the coiled snake may also be a lightly veiled *uroboros*. The serpent is frequently used by Osuna not only as a figure of prudence but also as one of change. In respect to *recogimiento* specifically, Osuna says that we must enter into our own hearts like a snake (*culebra*) that wants to moisten itself and discard its old skin. To do this, the snake bathes itself in a river and enters "por un angosto y áspero lugar" that scrapes away its old skin. Similarly, the contemplative bathes himself seven times in tears for his sins and enters, by the narrow door that is *recogimiento*, into his own heart. Here God and the soul find themselves alone (418).

The process of changing the skin is an obvious discarding of the old form, which is a necessary correlate to the statement we previously saw (Chapter IV) that the soul in contemplation awaits the infusion of a new form.[4]

The concept of change or "re-form" is again related to the serpent by Osuna in the Second Alphabet. Here, he says that self-contempt (*aborrecimiento de sí mismo*) is "botón de fuego que lanza fuera todo el hombre viejo y nos desuella dél como la culebra que pasando entre piedras ásperas deja la vieja vestidura" (fol. 51).[5]

A concise statement of the same theme is given by Osuna when he says that since the heart is the first organ formed by nature, it is the first that has to be "reformed."[6] The first step in reform is contrition, or self-contempt, which renders distasteful the old form, or "habit." (Cf. the form on the seal, Chapter IV.) Divesting oneself of it, however, is not easy.

The *culebra*, in Osuna, usually represents "transformation" or "transfiguration." The *áspide* is his usual serpent symbol of prudence. It is significant that in this treatise *culebra* is used where *áspide* would normally occur. The term *serpiente* is ambiguous; it will be discussed later.

Within the present context, the *culebra* may be taken as a symbol of "change of state," as well as of prudence. The particular change of state emphasized in this treatise is that of vaporization, or *sublimatio*. It appears in the simile of the hot steam from the boiling kettle that drives away flies, just as divine love operating within the soul drives away worldly temptations. In the preceding treatise, *mosquitos* are soul flying toward the divine Light, so this

---

[4] The term "infusion" is used by Osuna; it appears that he believed, with Aristotle, that form was created by the operation of the soul (from within) upon matter (Singer, *Anatomy*, 25).

[5] The snake's ability thus to change his form and to rejuvenate himself was adduced in ancient times as a major reason for identifying him with the sun and the Aeon. Hans Liesegang, "The Mystery of the Serpent," in *Pagan and Christian Mysteries*, 25.

[6] This concept of changing form by destroying the old one was put into pictorial form by Raphael in the fresco *Apollo and Marsyas*; the idea had already appeared in Dante (Wind, *Mysteries*, 143-44). Michaelangelo produced a Christian parallel in the flayed St. Bartholomew of the *Last Judgment*. The Saint holds in his hand the instrument of his flaying, a knife. A poem by Michaelangelo shows that he considered flaying a symbol of transformation through destruction, and he compares the process to the snake's shedding his skin on the rocks (Wind, *Mysteries*, 155).

figure is susceptible to two interpretations: divine love drives away the mundane, and raises the soul to the sublime. In short, just as Osuna says, the "fire" of love unites likes and separates unlikes.

Another reference to vaporization or to "boiling over" [7] is seen in the last chapter of treatise four, where the evacuation of the heart is ascribed to "el gran fervor" caused by the spirit of love.

Sublimation of a solid is referred to in the *incensario*, one of the figures occurring in the final list. The reference in all cases is to the sublimation of carnal desires into spiritual ones.

This particular type of change may have been selected because the concept occurs in Psalm 44, "Effundit cor meum verbum bonum." (Several items from this Psalm appear in treatise four; among them "la espada sobre el muslo," the sceptre [cf. *vara*], and the figure most typical of *recogimiento*: the nuptials of the king.) The idea of "effusion" appears here, to balance the concept of "infusion" that we discussed earlier.

Osuna apparently used this Psalm as one of his sources for treatise four. He may have selected it initially because of its number, which is the number four reduplicated. The text must have seemed to him extraordinarily apt. From it he could have taken the idea of "effusion," which accords so well with the liquid and pneumatic nature of the heart. This may, in turn, have suggested the choice of the other sublimation figures, and the text from Jeremiah, "spill out your heart like water...." As a final touch, the Psalm mentions the "word," which Osuna takes up again in the anecdote about St. Vincent. And, since it is a well-known psalm, the reader might be expected to think of it as he notices its figures; the memory of it then constitutes one "voice" in Osuna's polyphony.

Figures of will and decision. A figure intermediary between those of mutability and those of decision is the hawk (*gavilán*). It obviously represents the will, that "fills itself" with whatever is put before it, or "flies at anything it sees." As a member of the class called in the Bible *volátiles*, it suggests the notion of volatility seen in the preceding discussion. The changeability or volatility of

---

[7] The process of distillation is dominated by the zodiacal sign Virgo (Read, *Alchemist*, 14). This may have influenced Osuna in his choice of these figures; see the later section on symbols of the Virgin.

man is a natural attribute that can be put to good effect; it enables him to improve, says Osuna.

From Chapter II, we know that the intellect can place before the will a concept of the Divine, to which this hawk will fly. Osuna says later in this Alphabet that the soul "prende y arrebata a Dios," because God cannot refuse love, and he gives himself up like the heron (*garza*) when the falcon swoops (454).

Another figure linked to the concepts of mutability and of decision is the sword. In Osuna, the will may be represented by a knife, (*1 Abc.*, fol. 26); love may be also (*Convite*, fol. 66). Since the will has a selective operation, "querer y no querer," a cutting instrument is an apt symbol; it is especially suited to the irascible power, which rejects the harmful and "fights for the useful." Its operation is analogous to that of fire, the uniter of likes and separator of unlikes. Osuna persists in calling the flaming sword of paradise a knife (*cuchillo*), this is probably a clue to his intent.

To the alchemists, a knife or any cutting instrument represented fire (Read, *Alchemist*, 58-60). Its role in the process of distillation would be "separation," for example, and in fusing it would serve as the uniter.

The irascible power is the aspect of will concerned with rejection. Osuna emphasizes it in this treatise when he places it among the three major powers of the soul. In his first mention of the sword ("sobre el muslo por los temores nocturnos") he identifies it with irascibility. In the fable about St. Vincent, zeal for justice ("buena ira") also represents the power to reject.

In the same fable, as in the episode from Judges where the loaf of bread symbolized Gideon's sword, the power of God's word is equated to that of the sword. In the Fourth Alphabet, the word of God is a cutting instrument: contrition is "el corte hecho con la palabra de Dios, que corta los corazones;" it is also self-contempt (*4 Abc.*, 640), or penitence (*2 Abc.*, fol. 156). Self-contempt, we recall, was the "botón de fuego" that flayed the snake; so the Word may act as fire or sword.

Contrition is also called "ira sin pecado" (*4 Abc.*, 640). This is the aspect of it most evident in the anecdote; it is not a sin to be wrathful toward sin. St. Vincent's instructions to reprimand the "ravia" of the prideful judge can be read as a reprimand to the carnal, and prideful, nature: that is, as an injuction to contrition and reform. Wrath against sin is simply a negative phrasing of "zeal for justice," the "good wrath" of St. Thomas.

God's speech ("el habla de Dios") is also compared by Osuna to the fire that purifies the heart as a furnace purifies gold. Christ came to set the earth on fire; Jeremiah said he had this fire in his bones; in it the bush burned and was not destroyed (*4 Abc.*, 661). This fire may be the Eucharist (*Convite*, fol. 92).

In Isaiah 49:2, the word of God is called a sword; in Hebrews 4:12, it is said to be "más penetrante que espada de dos filos; y que entra y penetra hasta los pliegues del alma y del espíritu ... y discierne los pensamientos, y las intenciones del corazón."

The sword and the word both share the idea of "cutting" or selection, and both are compared to fire. Here, they point out that the contemplative must reject mundane and carnal preoccupations and turn his face toward the spiritual world.

The word or speech of God is the Logos, concealed in the human body of Christ or in the consecrated host (see Chapter VIII). It seems likely that He inspires contrition by the contrast between His performance while on earth, and ours. According to Osuna, in Christ we see what we should do, expressed in actions (*1 Abc.*, fol. 55). Osuna consels us to meditate the Passion before each exercise of *recogimiento*, it will be recalled. The Passion is also referred to as a knife (*1 Abc.*, fol. 159).

The double meaning of the praeteritio. At this point it seems advisable to look again at the *praeteritio*, in which the mundane soul was resoundingly cursed. We have already seen that the two-headed man did not simply represent the worldly priest; he exemplified a natural, God-given characteristic of human nature. The case of the untamed heart — the hawk — was similar; it symbolizes the will's ability to move toward any "good" that it perceives, and to capture it. These natural attributes may be used for good as well as evil; so that Osuna, under the pretext of excluding people with these traits, is in reality summoning all human souls to contrition, and with a promise of reward.

Further investigation shows that the "heartless" man and the hard-hearted one also have a potential for good. Osuna's usual figure for the "heartless" is the "paloma engañada que no tiene corazón." In the First Alphabet (Treatise I) this "dove" is the Christian who lets his heart be won by transitory and visible things. The world "steals" his heart. (This can be said because "más está el ánima donde ama que donde anima") (*3 Abc.*, 449). Elsewhere, however, Osuna points out that friends have only one heart in common; Christ melts human hearts and dissolves them into His. Under these circumstances it is good to be without a heart. Osuna says: "O si fuessemes como palomas engañadas con la dulzura de su cevo, y no tuviessemos corazón propio" (Osee 7.c) (*1 Abc.*, fol. 117).

The hard of heart are compared to diamonds. However, the blood of Christ has the property of goat's blood, it breaks diamonds; that is, it converts hardened sinners (*1 Abc.*, fol. 125).[8] This suggests the meditation of the Passion, which Osuna recommends, and also the property of baptismal water (which contains Christ's blood) to infuse charity (*4 Abc.*, 363-64). In visualizing the dying Christ, the heart is softened or moved to "compassion" (*1 Abc.*, fol. 72). Compassion is one of the three doors mentioned elsewhere through which Christ enters the heart. The others are contrition (discussed earlier) and love.

The diamond also has a magic attraction (*3 Abc.*, 322); grace is called a diamond because of this power of fascination (*3 Abc.*, 438). Osuna, in this treatise on mutability, expects the diamond to be appreciated in the light of all these attributes. It may attract the celestial forces, which are ever willing to come to the aid of the lost sheep or the wandering sinner.

The shrub (*retama*) in the desert also has its double nature. Not only may it symbolize the soul in the mundane world; or the *amor-humor* equation; elsewhere, it is the soul in the desert of *recogimiento*. This "zarza infructuosa" is the burning bush; Christ burns, in love, within it (*2 Abc.*, fol. 26). The *zarza* is also identified as the Cross (*5 Abc.*, fol. 75), and as the humanity of Christ (*1 Abc.*, fol. 31).

To the alchemists, flesh is "salt," as opposed to mercury, the "spirit" (Read, *Alchemist*, 7-8). To Osuna, salt may be worldly goods, that engender the desire for more (*5 Abc.*, fol. 102), or Christ, the divine Wisdom Who sweetened the waters of "the

---

[8] Osuna cites Pliny elsewhere to the effect that the blood of a goat drives out venoms and poisons and scares away serpents. Christ's blood, says Osuna, substitutes for the blood of all sacrificial animals (of Leviticus) including that of the goat (*1 Abc.*, fol. 118).

bitter sea of passions." Salt put into the mouth at baptism represents Christ (*5 Abc.*, fol. 2), the Word made flesh. "He who enters the world by two ways" may be interpreted as the Christian, who is re-born in baptism.

Since all the characteristics that Osuna explicitly condemns have a good as well as a bad aspect, we can see that his apparent rejection is, in fact, an invitation. The *praeteritio* is a formal reflection of the dualism expressed in so many of the items in this treatise — the soul itself, the two-headed man, and the hawk, for example. Such ambivalence arises naturally from Osuna's theory that all natural characteristics may be used for good or for evil, depending on the trajectory of the will. This gives man his mutable nature, which Osuna so strongly decries in this treatise, but which he calls elsewhere the power that enables all men to rise to the sublime. The *praeteritio* does, then, invite all men to become pure in heart, so that they may see God. The "letter" of the *praeteritio* condemns, but the spirit offers life.

The castle, the Terrestrial Paradise and the Ark of the Covenant. [9] If the heart is properly guarded, it is like a castle (in Osuna's usage, a fortified place). Its three guardians — reason, irascibility and will — are figured in the items found in the terrestrial paradise and in the Ark of the Covenant.

In this paradise is the fountain of Grace that divides itself into four streams, identified by Osuna as the cardinal virtues that combat the four passions.

This fountain elsewhere represents Christ, and the four streams are His tears, mortal sweat, blood, and the water from His side, which is the water of baptism (*1 Abc.*, fol. 45). Tears of contrition are a reiterated baptism (*3 Abc.*, 436); so such tears come to have a power like that of baptismal water; they frighten the devil (*2 Abc.*, fol. 71); they are also the softening agent that enables the snake to change his skin; they soften the hard heart and irrigate the sterile earth of the soul. Moreover, they are the flood that raises Noah's ark (the contemplative) to the height of contemplation (*3 Abc.*, 436).

---

[9] These are all emblems of the Blessed Virgin; her role will be discussed in a later section.

Water, according to Osuna, is the most fecund of elements, and the one that most impregnates the earth. For this reason it is a figure of mercy. The fountain in Paradise is the mercy of God in which souls are again baptized (*5 Abc.*, fol. 162). Since baptism in new infusion of "soul" this statement lends some weight to the hypothesis that Osuna identified *ánima* with liquids.

The tree of life in paradise, identified as spiritual wisdom or the taste of contemplation (*saber* and *sabor* are played upon by Osuna [*3 Abc.*, 373]) is also a symbol of the Cross, Christ Himself, and of the Virgin. Osuna says that Christ is the tree (Daniel 4.b) in the middle of the earth, which reached up to heaven. Its fruit is the sustenance of all flesh, which, according to Osuna, illustrates the fecundity of Christ (*1 Abc.*, fol. 107).

More specifically, a long theological tradition identifies the tree of life as the Cross, and the fountain as the baptismal font, which derives its efficacy from the Crucifixion.[10] In this light, Osuna's comments on the tree and the fountain become clear. We noted earlier that the blood and water from Christ's side is the baptismal water; the wound is therefore the font. The tree is fecund, because Christ's blood in the font generates all Christians; they are the fruits of this tree.

The earthly paradise is related to the figure of the garden of King Asuero, and the country-house of Solomon. These are the garden of the Beloved in the Canticle. This garden is human nature, where God, "eating the fruit of His apple trees," incorporates into Himself the "predestined" (*1 Abc.*, fol. 163).

In the garden of the sepulchre — which is the heart contemplating the Passion — Christ is the tree of life whose fruit is Grace. The sepulchre is empty when self-will is ejected to leave room for Christ (as it is in *recogimiento*) (*1 Abc.*, fol. 172). This would justify calling the heart a sepulchre of Christ, as Osuna does in the final list of figures.[11] To this sepulchre comes the Magdalen (the contemplative soul), seeking Him (*3 Abc.*, 480).

---

[10] Hugo Rahner, S. J., "The Christian Mystery and the Pagan Mysteries," *Pagan and Christian Mysteries*, 203.

[11] However, in the context of this chapter, Osuna may have in mind the following passage from St. Paul [Rom. 6:4, 5, 6]: "En efecto, en el bautismo hemos quedado sepultados con él, muriendo al pecado: a fin de que así como Cristo resucitó de muerte a vida para gloria del Padre, así

SOME MAJOR FIGURES OF TREATISE IV 131

If the figure of the earthly paradise or garden of the sepulchre is construed to refer to the meditation on the Passion, we should recall that this exercise is designed to help collect wandering thoughts (*1 Abc.*, fol. 22), as the Good Shepherd collects lost sheep. (This figure occurs immediately after that of the hawk; sequential order is often significant in Osuna). The canons of the foregoing figures suggest that contemplation of the Passion is viewed as a renewed baptism. Osuna says elsewhere that it can be so considered, because the Passion is the origin and source of baptism. Such contemplation is a bath of renovation in which the soul, like a prudent *culebra*, washes itself, so that, in the softness of heart so acquired, it can easily remove the old skin and dress itself in the "new man," created by the Passion in the image of God (*2 Abc.*, fol. 134).

To the contemplative, the cross is the tree in whose shade sits the Bride (Cant. 2.g). Its fruit is Christ, the bread and wine (*1 Abc.*, fol. 37), or the "taste" of Divinity. The contemplative who eats is himself "eaten", that is, he is absorbed into the Divinity within him. The soul in contemplation becomes like the snake that eats himself; when he enters his own heart, he is absorbed by the God within, whom he in turn absorbs. "El que come mi carne y bebe mi sangre, permanesce en mi y yo en el (Joa. 6.f)" (*2 Abc.*, fol. 29).

This, certainly, is a reference to the Eucharist. Citing St. Augustine, Osuna says that the tree of life is the Eucharist, "porq̃ no quiso nr̃o señor que el hombre viuiesse en el parayso terrenal sin misterios de cosas spirituales representadas corporalmente." The fount in Paradise represents baptism (*5 Abc.*, fol. 115).

The Eucharistic wine is, of course, Christ's blood, by which we participate in, and are joined to, Christ. By means of it we recover the grace given in baptism. The water mixed with the wine signifies

---

también procedamos nosotros con nuevo tenor de vida. 5) Que si hemos sido injertados con él por medio de la representación de la muerte, igualmente lo hemos de ser representando su resurrección. 6) haciéndonos cargo que nuestro hombre viejo fue crucificado juntamente con él, para que sea destruido en nosotros el cuerpo del pecado, y ya no sirvamos más al pecado." (*Recogimiento* itself is also called by Osuna "sepultarse") (*3 Abc.*, 425). Notice that in the Biblical passage "injertados" suggests the tree also. This passage is cited by Osuna in *6 Abc.*, fol. 45. Christ's resurrection is a figure of our spiritual one (*5 Abc.*, fol. 117).

death; it shows that the mass represents Christ's history "from the Supper to the Cross" (*5 Abc.*, fol. 121).

In this context, the hollow altar is the place where free will sacrifices the bull (pride); wrath (the ram), lust and evil desires (goats), with the knife of continence. The host in this sacrifice is prayer (*5 Abc.*, fols. 35-36). Elsewhere, the host is the Incarnate Word, Who enters into us to unite us to Him (*5 Abc.*, fol. 115).

In the Ark of the Covenant, the *vara castigadora* (*vara de Aarón*) corresponds to the sword in the earthly paradise. We should recall, now, that the sword (irascibility) could manifest itself as a word, in the anecdote about St. Vincent. This sword is connected with the sword from the mouth of Christ the Judge, *Verbo de Dios* [Apoc. 19:15]. Here Christ is to rule the peoples with a rod (*vara*) of iron.

The rod, however, may not always be the symbol of negative judgment. The word of God is also a rod or sceptre of gold, symbol of the indulgence of King Assuerus (Est. 5.a). In this Biblical chapter, Esther wins the king's good will to the extent of his promising her half the kingdom, if she likes. Assuerus, says Osuna, is a figure of Christ; Esther may represent the suppliant soul (*5 Abc.*, fol. 48). A text from Isaiah [11:4] sums up the role of the Judge: "Juzgará a los pobres con justicia, y herirá la tierra con la vara de su boca." In medieval and renaissance art, Christ the Judge is often represented with a sword and a lily proceeding from His mouth, representing condemnation and mercy.[12] The rod symbolizes, then, the selective or discriminatory function of the will, as did the sword. A green branch in the mouth also represents the Eucharist (*Convite*, fol. 92).

Manna is identified with the flame. This is *codicia*, or the desire for the pleasing, and is a figure of the ecstatic union, or "gusto de la vida eterna," that occurs in contemplation (*3 Abc.*, 346). Osuna says that the Israelites did not receive manna until the flour from Egypt was all gone. This flour symbolizes the consolation derived from created things, from which one must separate himself completely in contemplation. Manna also stands for grace, which is

---

[12] Manuel Trens, *María: Iconografía de la Virgen en el arte español* (Madrid, 1946), 277.

God's love coming down to the soul (*4 Abc.*, 684). It comes down like manna to those who are in the desert of this life (*3 Abc.*, 346) or in the "desert" of contemplation.

The tablets of the Law are identified with the cherub, or the rational faculty, that discerns and shows the will what is good, and what is to be avoided ("Thou shalt" and "Thou shalt not").

The figure of the Ark is a reduplication of the principles shown in the cherub, flame, and sword of the earthly paradise. These principles, however, are shown to apply to God as well as to the soul. He judges, condemns the carnal, accepts the spiritual, and sends His love downward to be united with the upward-rising soul.

The Ark itself is compared by Osuna to the contemplative, who "never leaves the interior of the temple"; (p. 422) that is, he keeps God always present in his thoughts. The rod is desire; its flower is the joy of "complacencia" or fulfillment (*4 Abc.*, 525). The *vara*, therefore, is not only the will that selects but the will that seeks; the uniter as well as the separater.

In the *Convite*, Osuna calls the body an ark; the four walls are the four elements of which it is composed. The soul is the golden vessel within it (fols. 101-102). In *Norte* (fol. 133), the soul is the *arca de Dios*; manna represents the will; the tablets, intellect; the rod, memory which stretches from the past toward the future (compare the interpretation of the Janus-figure).

The Ark is also the heart of Jesus, in the temple of His body. The wound in His side is the narrow door into this "abbreviated paradise," which is the intellect of God — the Logos. Into this heart the contemplative enters (*1 Abc.*, fol. 117). The Ark, therefore, also symbolizes contemplation, where the mysteries ("archana") are contained. The contemplative, like the cherubim, must embrace this *arca*. Osuna refers us to Richard of St. Victor for further explanations of this figure (*4 Abc.*, 656-657). Christ's heart is also the Ark of the "true Noah"; its wound is the window from which the dove (the church) came forth (*1 Abc.*, fol. 117).

In comparing both the heart of man and the heart of Jesus to the Ark of the Covenant and to paradise, Osuna points to the fact that the human soul is made in the image of the Divine (he mentions this at the beginning of the treatise), and also that it is within the Divine when it enters into itself. This is possible in view of the intellectual nature of the heart: the Logos has, in His heart, a concept of the individual, and the individual has a concept of the Logos. In this sense, each possesses the other, and each may be said to "conceive" the other. Therefore the term "Ark" is also applied to the Eucharist (*Convite*, fol. 18) in which Christ and man reciprocally "contain" each other. In an easter play by Juan del Encina, "arca" refers to the tabernacle in which the consecrated host is kept.[13]

Since the Ark of the "true Noah" was also a figure of the heart in one quotation, we begin to suspect that the next major figure, the ship, is intended to suggest Noah's Ark. The ship follows close upon the "arca del Señor," and such a correspondence of titles would be difficult for Osuna to resist. The ship of Treatise IV is almost certainly identified as Noah's Ark by the appearance in the same treatise of the rainbow ("el arco de la amistad puesto en las nubes de las lágrimas") — the sign promised to Noah.

The ship. The ship is a figure with many tenors; it may be the world (a ship that leaves no wake) (*2 Abc.*, fol. 15), or the Cross on which we traverse the sea of life (*1 Abc.*, fol. 37), or the spirit of wisdom, which goes by sea like Solomon's treasure fleet, and reaches "Dios purísimo" (*5 Abc.*, fol. 85).

In this treatise, Osuna identifies the "navecilla" as the body, the heart being the *bomba*. Elsewhere, spiritual exercises are called *navecillas* in which "cada justo con su familia interior y mundo menor debe salvarse" (an apparent reference to the Deluge). "Sacrifiquen á Dios sacrificio de alabanza, y denuncien las obras dél en alegría los que descienden a la mar en naos, haciendo operación en las muchas aguas; estos vieron las obras del Señor y las maravillas dél en lo profundo" (Psal. CVI, cited by Osuna). Osuna says that in the exercise of contemplation you will see the marvels of the Lord in the depths of the heart (*3 Abc.*, 368).

Besides representing a spiritual exercise, the ship may stand for the heart itself, sailing to God on a sea of tears. Also, the contemplative may be the Ark, lifted by a flood of tears to

---

[13] Juan del Encina, 1496, in N. D. Shergold, *A History of the Spanish Stage from Medieval Times until the End of the Seventeenth Century* (Oxford, 1967), 27.

the height of contemplation (*3 Abc.*, 436). Or the Ark may be *la bienaventuranza*; the possession of God (*6 Abc.*, fol. 62).

The tenors of this figure supply us with several references to the Deluge, to be assessed with the baptismal figure that has been discussed in relation to the fountain and the tree. It seems likely that this ship is yet another reference to the "mystery of wood and water" (Rahner, "Christian Mystery," 203 and n.), that is, the sacrament of baptism. "The Ark by which man was saved is a symbol of the Cross," Rahner says (200). He cites in part the first Epistle of Peter (3:20-22), in which the Ark is identified as a figure of baptism. Verse twenty notes that a few persons were saved from the flood in the Ark; the next verse reads: "La cual era figura del bautismo de ahora, el cual de una manera semejante os salva a vosotros; no con quitar las manchas de la carne, sino justificando la conciencia para con Dios por la virtud de la resurrección de Jesucristo; ..."

Into this context fits another of Osuna's interpretations of the rainbow; it is the crucified Christ (*2 Abc.*, fol. 95).

The connection of the Crucifixion to baptism is symbolically expressed in the Greek liturgy by the dipping of a cross into the baptismal water; in the Roman liturgy a candle is used; it also is a symbol of Christ crucified (Rahner, "Christian Mystery," 205-6).

As if to emphasize the factor of concealment in his treatment of the Ark, Osuna has utilized in this treatise many items to which the word "arca" can be applied. Besides the two already mentioned, the thoracic cavity is called by Osuna an *arca*. It thus becomes like the tabernacle, and the heart is "vaso de oro lleno del maná de la gracia celestial, puesto en el arca de tu pecho" (final list of figures, Treatise IV). Another type of *arca* is a "depósito de aguas"; into this general category would fit the bilge of the ship and perhaps even the fonts of paradise and of baptism.

A furnace for re-heating glass vessels is also an *arca*; the furnace is a figure of Treatise IV, and the meek, in Treatise III, are called glass vessels. Since Osuna mentions furnaces and their operations with surprising frequency and some knowledge, he may have known that the term *arca* was applied to one type.

The hollow altar "que no era macizo" could be called an *arca*, in the general sense. Perhaps Osuna's insistence on its hollowness indicates that he intended it should be.

The heart itself, as a closed, hollow container, can easily be compared to an *arca*, which has this general meaning. Once the heart is viewed as a container it can then be named for what it contains, so that an even wider variety of figures becomes possible. A glance at the figures of Treatise IV will show numerous "containers" of fire (love), of fluids, things, and people. This is all possible because the heart, as the seat of intellect, "contains" anything the mind can conceive.

Analogous to the heart as a material container of divinity is the body as a material container of the soul. The tenor of most of the figures in Treatise IV is divinity contained within humanity. This may refer to Christ, the Word made flesh, or to the soul in the body, or to the presence of Christ in the heart of the contemplative.

Once this canon was established, Osuna could select from many possible figures those that would convey what he wanted to tell us about *recogimiento*.

In choosing to include the "arco de la amistad," Osuna was probably influenced by the resemblance of *arco* to *arca* and by the fact that the rainbow provides a clue to the identity of Noah's Ark, in case the unsuspecting reader has missed it.

Chapter VIII

AN ANAGOGICAL LEVEL:
ITS REVELATION AND ITS PURPOSE

Symbols of the virgin. The heart is called an ark because it is a container, and because it holds thoughts of divine things it is analogous to other containers of such things. The prototype of the "material container of divinity" is, of course, the Blessed Virgin. Several of the figures of the heart in this treatise are emblems of the Virgin; among them are the earthly paradise ("el vientre de la virgen"), the fountain, the tree of life, the closed garden, the rod of Aaron,[1] the ship ("arca del diluvio"), the house (*domus Dei*), the Ark of the Covenant, the vessel (*vaso*) of gold, the city of God, even the two-headed person: *janua* ("puerta") *coeli*. Osuna also names as symbols of Mary the garden of King Ahasuerus, the window of the Ark (from which the dove came forth), and the green thorn-bush (*zarza*) undamaged by the fire of carnal passion (*Norte*, fol. 24).

Another figure of the Virgin is the widow of IV Kings 4, whom Osuna identifies in this treatise as Spiritual Wisdom.

In the scriptural story, the woman of IV Kings 4 is in want, and her creditors are about to carry away her two sons into

---

[1] Trens says that every occurrence in the Bible of the word *virga* (staff, rod, *vara*) was customarily read as an allusion to the Virgin (*virgo*). He gives a list of these passages and their interpretations, compiled by no less an authority than Aquinas (*María*, 552-53). For the identification of the emblems of the Virgin I am also indebted to Trens (153-54 and 163-64).

A modern novena to Our Lady of Guadalupe identifies the Virgin also with the rainbow and the diamond. *El devocionario para todos* (El Paso, Revista Católica, 1962), 317, 323.

slavery. She owns nothing but a little oil. Elisha has her borrow vessels from the neighbors; and through a miracle, he increases her oil so much that it fills all the available vessels.

Osuna advises us to offer our empty hearts to the widow; whe will put in a drop of her grace and it will increase until the heart is full. This grace or "sabiduría" is received best, he says, when the heart is most empty, so that it can be filled and occupied by the operation of the Holy Spirit. The most perfect example of this is the Virgin, who conceived the Son of God.

In order to appreciate the analogy between contemplation and the Annunciation one must know that Osuna believes the Virgin conceived Christ mentally before she conceived Him corporally (*1 Abc.*, fol. 106). Osuna cites St. Augustine to the effect that she was more blessed in conceiving the faith (the idea) than the flesh (*1 Abc.*, fol. 121). Osuna adds that she carried Christ in her heart (her thoughts) as she carried Him in her body.

The idea that the mental concept is a greater blessing than the physical conception is founded on the passage from Luke (11: 27, 28) (cited by Osuna in folio 121 above) in which the woman exclaimed to Jesus: "Bienaventurado el vientre que te llevó y los pechos que te alimentaron."

And He answered: "Bienaventurados más bien los que escuchan la palabra de Dios y la ponen en práctica."

The last is the objective of the contemplative. Osuna says in the Third Alphabet that the Virgin was in *recogimiento* when "Dios ... se infundió en sus entrañas, para obrar realmente lo que cada dia obra espiritualmente en las ánimas sanctas en que se transforma" (430). It is apparent from this that the material and the spiritual conception are considered analogous, and that mental conception is of daily occurrence.

It is now possible to see why the Virgin is cited as the model of contemplatives (this occurs several times in the Alphabets), and also why the heart is compared to her emblems. The experience of *recogimiento* is that of "conceiving" Christ mentally, in order to put the Word of God into practice. In the case of the Blessed Virgin, this spiritual event became a material reality: the Word, or Concept, was made flesh.

According to Philo, the "mother" of the uncreated Logos is Wisdom (Inge, "Logos," 133-38). Inasmuch as Osuna has identified the widow of IV Kings 4 as Spiritual Wisdom; it would appear that he is acquainted with this tradition. Since experience of the Divine, through contemplation, is Wisdom, and Mary is its model, she is very closely identified with the Wisdom that is the Mother of the Word. Trens says that there was a notion prevalent in the Middle Ages and Renaissance of the Virgin as "pre-existent": that is, existing in the mind of God eternally. In iconography, this Virgin is depicted as the woman in the Apocalypse (*María*, 56-57).

Mary's role in giving material form [2] to the Logos is analogous to that of the contemplative when he translates his concept of Christ into actions. It is the eruption of spiritual forces into the world of matter. [3]

With this in mind, we can glimpse the really crucial role of the Virgin in this treatise, which began with an evocation of the shrub in the salty earth — a figure of the hardness and intransigence of matter. Mary is the channel through which this world is penetrated and vivified by spiritual forces. The contemplative essays to play this same part.

The Blessed Virgin, like the *arca*, appears in this treatise in disguise more often than under her own name. Osuna uses approximately a dozen of her emblems; he names her twice.

---

[2] Relevant to the analogy between mental and physical conception is Aristotle's theory, influential in Christian theology, that the female contributed all matter to the new organism, the male all soul or "form." This last is communicated mysteriously, without any real necessity for physical contact (Singer, *Anatomy*, 24-25). Panofsky (*Iconology*, 142) says that a relationship between the words *mater* and *materia* was seen. I would deduce that the latter idea is a reflection of Aristotle's notion.

[3] Osuna says: "La recreación del hombre había de ser conforme a su creación para que hubiese correspondencia y semejanza de la reformación a la formación. Cuando Dios formó al hombre primero dijo: Hagamos un hombre a nuestra imagen y semejanza que se pueda enseñorear de todas las cosas que hemos creado. Esto mismo parece haber dicho el Hijo de Dios cuando redimió al hombre, pues quiere que el hombre redimido sea semejante y conforme a la imagen de Jesu Christo, que es la vida trabajosa y llagada que vivió en este mundo por nuestro amor" (6 *Abc.*, fol. 53).

The "spiritual body" is the sum of one's works (5 *Abc.*, fol. 114), not the external shape.

In the "merit" of these works, there is "material and form;" the materials are human effort, and the form is Grace (5 *Abc.*, fol. 127).

Because she is the bringer of saving grace, the Virgin is compared to any "vessel" or instrument of grace, including the vessel of manna, the Ark of Noah, the Ark of the Covenant, and even Aaron's rod that smote the rock, bringing the saving waters. (Christ is the Rock; the waters are grace.) (Trens, *María*, 552). Her emblems used in this treatise fit either this aspect, or her role as a "container" of divinity, or both.

In the final list of figures that Osuna gives us in this treatise, the "chamber of the real Elisha" is also an allusion to the Virgin. The reference is again to IV Kings 4; in this second story the barren Sunamitess came to Elisha's room to pray for the grace of conception; her wish was miraculously granted through the power of Elisha's words. She had a son who died and was resuscitated by the prophet. The text is an obvious parallel to the life of Christ and Mary; Osuna identifies the Sunamitess as a figure of the Virgin in the First Alphabet (fol. 175).

Almost as apparent is the analogy between this story and the contemplative experience. The heart, of course, is the "room" into which the soul enters to pray for the concept.

The text of IV Kings 4 offers two stories applicable to the theme of *recogimiento*; typically, Osuna chose to use the one in which the allegorical value was harder to discern, and to refer to the more obvious one by an unobtrusive figure.

Osuna probably hit upon this scriptural text because of its number, which corresponds to the number of the treatise, the number of chambers within the heart, the four passions, and other sets of four that occur here.[4] He may have been influenced by

---

[4] Four is also a feminine number, according to Philo. As it represents the cube or solid (Thorndike, *Magic*, I, 355-57) it coul be construed as representing an *arca*. (According to Rahner, the number eight, or four doubled, is the numerical symbol for baptism, because eight people were saved in the Ark. Eight is the number that represented the cube to many people ["Christian Mystery," 202]). In Plato the cube is the geometric figure that represents earth (*Timaeus*, 57). Also, Plato identifies the number 4 as the middle of a series — the series of 7 harmonic intervals into which the world-soul is divided (*Tim.*, 25). These intervals are repeated in the human soul (39). Four is the middle of a series in the seven-note musical scale (Roger Bragard, "L'harmonie des sphères selon Boèce," *Speculum*, IV, 1929, 213). There is a remote possibility that this might explain Osuna's calling the fourth treatise a "middle" term; numbers and letters may designate musical notes.

numeralogical considerations when he chose to refer to IV Kings 4 and Psalm 44. A similar concern may have inspired him to call the fourth treatise the second within a series of three. A reader more familiar than I with the procedures of numerology might have detected in this some clue to numerical manipulations.

Out discussion of the figures so far has brought to light certain general motifs. One is the dual nature of man; or rather his capacity to use his human potential either for good or for evil. Another is contrition, the desire to change old customs for better ones. An important theme is that of death, figured in the act of contemplation itself, in the Flood, in the "chaos before Creation" that Osuna mentions, and in the sepulchre. Introduced concurrently with the theme of death is that of birth; this is made possible through the coincidence of these tenors in several figures, especially that of Noah's Ark. Other manifestations of the motif of conception and birth are found in other emblems of the Virgin, and in the outright nuptial and birth figures.

Knowing the rationale of *recogimiento*, we can recognize what we see here as a symbolic representation of the psychological drama enacted in the state thereof. The contemplative, inspired by a desire to reform his life after the model of Christ's, "dies" to the carnal world of the senses. In this death the soul separates itself from the body sufficiently to enter the domain of the spirit, as Christ did when he passed from mortal to eternal life. The spiritual world of pure ideas is the mind of the Logos; that is, the heart of Jesus, for the mind is in the heart. In this heart, through the generative power of Christ's blood, the "concept" takes form and is born into the world as the new Christian, modeled after Christ.

Since generation consits of the infusion of soul or "form," a mental "transformation" can easily be spoken of as a "new birth." Similarly, the abandonment of all ideas and "forms" in the mind, which is the injunction of this treatise ("Desembaraza el corazón y vacía todo lo criado") is a reversion to the state of formlessness, or death.

Because the infusion of soul is looked upon as a spiritual event, it could logically be argued that in physical generation the mental concept was prior to the material conception. Perhaps this is why Osuna declares that the mental conception of Christ came first.[5]

Some cosmic concepts suggested by the figures. The figure of the serpent is one that requires further comment in the light of the theme of death and rebirth. Osuna has already told us that the *culebra* is a figure of the "shedding" of the old form that takes place when the contemplative enters into his own heart. This separation from the old form is followed, as we should expect, by a joining, for love separates unlikes and joins likes. This joining is expressed in the serpent figure in the First Alphabet (fol. 117), where Christ is like Moses' serpent that swallowed and incorporated into itself the other serpents made by "art." Christ melts hearts and joins them to Himself.

The serpents "made by art" are individuals; Christ the Logos is the "Art" of the Father, the Art by which all things are made (*1 Abc.*, fols. 100-101). He is therefore the Maker of the indi-

---

[5] Since the figures of this treatise resolve themselves into symbols of rejection of the world, love for the spiritual, union and conception, they could be depicted in pictorial form as the Apocalyptic Virgin. She is described as standing on the moon, and dressed in sunlight (Apoc. 12). Osuna says she is the Christian soul who despises the moon (sensuality) and appreciates the sun (*5 Abc.*, fol. 93). This representation of the Immaculate Conception is frequently referred to by Trens, who shows numerous plates, almost all of which include a serpent (usually interpreted as Satan), entwined about the moon. In a painting by Zurbarán (seventeenth century, in Sevilla) the serpent is replaced by a heart, which Trens does not explain (Trens, *María*, 181). In my opinion, this painting forms an iconographic summary of the contents of the treatise we have been discussing, especially since the scene is nocturnal, and *recogimiento* is the "dark night" of the senses, in which *alumbramiento* takes place. Perhaps some earlier representation of this *Immaculada* was one of the images that inspired, in Osuna, great devotion, and it might have guided his selection of figures for this treatise. Or, in his turn, Zurbarán could have been influenced by ideas from Osuna, or similar views drawn from a source I have not identified.

A literary reference to such a figure is seen in the sonnet "A la Asunción de la Virgen María" by Pedro Espinosa (1578-1650): "Por manto el sol, la luna por chapines / llegó la Virgen a la empírea sala..." (Elías L. Rivers, *Renaissance and Baroque Poetry of Spain* (New York, 1966), 259.

In modern devotions addressed to the Virgin of Guadalupe there are references to the Apocalyptic Virgin; in this case the moon and a winged seraph are beneath her feet ("Gozos," *Devocionario para todos*, 329-331). The winged seraph can certainly be interpreted as a symbol of volatility; it may represent this attribute of *espíritu* as distinguished from *ánima*, which is usually related to the moon.

vidual, and when the contemplative is "melted" or "eaten" by the Logos, he is re-incorporated into his Originator.

The serpent, to Osuna, often represents the good soul. When Christ is figured in the burning bush, He is called the refuge of saints and sinners, as the bush is to *culebras y lagartos* (*1 Abc.*, fol. 31). (This statement may have been in Osuna's mind when he placed the figure of the prudent snake in Treatise IV, along with the burning bush.)

The *culebras* who are saints are swallowed up, according to Osuna and incorporated into Christ. In the First Alphabet, Osuna says that Moses' upraised serpent is a figure of Christ's death on the Cross, a death caused by "la serpiente antigua." This passage is followed by a statement that Christ is the Priest who sacrifices Himself (*1 Abc.*, fol. 64). (This may account in part for the inclusion of the altar among the figures of Treatise IV.)

The first of these passages makes it appear that Christ's death was caused by the devil, whom we associate with "la serpiente antigua." This is incompatible with the second statement, however, which makes Christ the determiner of His own death. The second idea is the one that prevails in Osuna's doctrine, and is a principle embodied in the sacrifice of the Mass. However, if Christ sacrifices Himself, then He Himself could be "la serpiente antigua." (The brazen serpent raised by Moses [Num. 21:8] is identified by John [3:14] as a figure of Christ.) There is a parallel between this idea of Him and the concept of the Aeon that was current among both pagan and Christian writers of late antiquity. The Aeon was symbolized by the snake with his tail in his mouth, because he eats himself and is renewed, like the year.

If the death of Christ was to Osuna the death of an Aeon, a new phase of time should immediately occur. And in fact, he says that Good Friday was the "end of the year" (*1 Abc.*, fol. 77). Moreover, a new creation took place with the Passion; Osuna specifies the new "works of the six days" (*1 Abc.*, fol. 27). Of course, the Age of Grace was inaugurated, and our present era began its year enumeration.

Time and eternity: universal and particular. To the family of Aeon or "time" symbols also belong Janus, the two-headed man, and the wheel (Panofsky, *Iconology*, 71-74 and footnotes), as well as the four winds, which in the Christian tradition of the Aeon represent the four angels that "with a great sound of a trumpet, ... shall gather together his elect from the four winds...." (Matt. 24:31) (Leisegang, "Serpent", 36). We have here a secondary set of meanings for the wheel with four faces, and the four winds, identified by Osuna in this treatise as the soul with its four passions.

According to Leisegang ("Serpent," 37-38), the concept of Christ as the Aeon was already present in New Testament times, and persisted into the late middle ages. The serpent with his tail in his mouth (the *uroboros*) symbolizes Alpha and Omega, the beginning and the end. This abstraction — the idea of a combined origin and end — fits not only the Aeon who swallws himself, but also the concept of the serpent that swallows up its children.[6] It also suggests the alphabetical format.

The uroboros also represents the mercurial principle, the power to produce a change of state. Some comments on the nature of the Logos have a bearing on this and other figures of our treatise. The Logos is, to Philo, the idea of ideas. (Compare Osuna, "Allí [en Él] mejor que en dechado están las ideas de todas las cosas y las razones seminales de todo lo posible" (*3 Abc.*, 442). In Him, the undivided One is divided into many finite manifestations. He is both the intelligible world and the real life of the real world. Philo calls the Logos the "cutter," citing the passage (Gen. 15:10) in which Abraham divides the animals in two. He produces creation by dichotomy (that is, He is the Unity that creates multiplicity) and He is also the Joiner (Wind, *Mysteries*, 166). As such, the Logos Himself could well be represented by the two-headed man who looks both to the world of universals and to that of particulars. As "cutter," or divider of the universe into particulars, the Logos could be figured in the sword.

As the Joiner of all creation, which is dissolved and incorporated into Him, He is represented by the serpent and the Tree

---

[6] This is one of the ideas associated with the myth of Saturn swallowing his children (Panofsky, *Iconology*, 78-79). Can the complex symbolism associated with the serpent be related to the *tarasca*, the Corpus Christi dragon? Also, the eagle and serpent emblem of Mexico acquires a new sigrificance if considered in the light of Osuna's symbolism. Early Franciscans in Mexico — Osuna may have been their chief — must have been struck by indigenous representations of the plumed serpent.

of Life. In the one case he eats his children; in the other he eats his own apples, as Osuna has said.⁷

As both cutter and joiner He was represented by Osuna in fire; spiritual baptism is a baptism by fire. (*Convite*, fol. 94). As the seminal force that generates individuals, He is figured in the Word, in the alphabet, and in the heart and blood itself, containing the forces of love and of generation.

Baptism. The most comprehensive figures of Treatise IV are, however, the earthly paradise and the Ark of Noah. These suggest the sacrament of baptism, which we know to be a symbolic death and resurrection. According to modern authority, baptism is a symbol of the flood, of death, resurrection, the nuptials of Christ, and the conception and birth of the church.⁸

Osuna has said that the passion of Christ is also his espousal. The sacrament of baptism is the only "figure" in which the death, nuptials and rebirth theme is completely represented. If we were to adopt this motif as the principal one, we should see if it helps us to account for figures still unexplained.

The term "consistorio" of God (applied in Treatise IV to the heart) is applied by Osuna also to baptism. In addition, baptism is "el primer desposorio." (*4 Abc.*, 247).

Baptism is also compared to the Annunciation. Osuna says that just as the Holy Spirit came to Mary so that Christ would be conceived, so the spirit descends upon the baptismal waters to cause the conception of the "spiritual man" (*4 Abc.*, 362-63). Baptism is the "nativity" of the Christian (*1 Abc.*, fol. 122).

The baptismal water is the water and blood from Christ's side. This is the blood of the bird sacrificed over "living water" [Lv. 14], with which a living bird is stained. The sacrifice is for the cure of the leper (*1 Abc.*, fols. 45, 46). The leper of this

---

⁷ Leisegang says ("Serpent", 17) that with the birth of Phanes (the Orphic Aeon), Heaven and earth were split apart; however, the great Serpent still connected them. Wind (*Mysteries*, 27) shows a fifteenth century diagram of the spheres, each identified with a musical mode, and with a three-headed serpent stretching from Heaven to earth. (In Daniel 4b it is the Tree of Life that joins earth to Heaven.)

⁸ Daniel J. Sullivan, "Symbolism in Catholic Worship," *Religious Symbolism*, ed. by F. Ernest Johnson (Inst. for Religious and Social Studies: Jewish Theological Seminary of America, 1955), 49.

figure is the mundane man, the sinner, still suffering from what St. Peter called "las manchas de la carne."

According to Osuna, the act of baptism cannot be repeated, but it can be renewed in its origin (which is the Passion), by meditation. This is the *lauatorio de renouacion* in which our soul should bathe itself like the prudent *culebra*, so that in the resultant softness of heart the old skin may be cast away and the New Christian form put on. Osuna cites St. Paul in this passage: Ef. 4, Tit. 3, Col. 3 (*2 Abc.*, fol. 134). In these chapters from St. Paul, the theme of rebirth is to be found, but without mention of the serpent.

Although there are many suggestions in this treatise of the sacrament of communion, I believe that we must take seriously Osuna's statement that the Mass represents events from the Supper until the death on the Cross. Baptism seems to include the death, resurrection, nuptial and generation figures more adequately. Reading the figures in the treatise alone, I believe that they reveal an exposition of the experience of *recogimiento*: contrition and compassion evoked by contemplation of the Passion; a flight into the spiritual world, equivalent to death; and the infusion of a new form or "soul" — which is a new pattern of thought and activity.

Elsewhere, Osuna has said that to meditate on the Passion is to eat the body and drink the blood of Christ in memory (*3 Abc.*, 442). He has also said that such meditation may be a baptism: "Every sacrament represents the Passion which gave it its virtue," and everything contemplated as a representation of the Passion comes to be a sacrament (*2 Abc.*, 134). In the *Fourth Alphabet*, the same figure (Rebecca) represents both the baptized Christian and the devout soul who "descends to the baptismal font when he humbles himself to receive it" [God's favor] (chap. 16). It appears that Osuna, in Treatise IV, indicates that *recogimiento* is to be viewed as a renewed spiritual baptism.

Osuna, citing Dionysius, calls baptism "sacramento de iluminacion" (*6 Abc.*, fol. 82). The idea postulated here may have a bearing on the term "alumbrado" ("illuminated," "delivered" or "born") as applied to religious enthusiasts of the sixteenth century. St. Paul [Col. 2,3] speaks of moral regeneration as putting on the "new man" after death and resuscitation in baptism. This sacrament is a spiritual circumcision that brings pardon for sin, by the power of the Cross. No one should, therefore, be condemned because of his food or drink, or celebration of holidays, etc.; these rituals were only shadows of which Christ is the reality (Col. 2).

St. Paul follows the theme of rebirth to its logical conclusion. Some of his statements have a direct bearing on remarks made by Osuna.

> Haced morir, pues, los miembros del hombre terreno que hay en vosotros: la fornicación, la impureza, las pasiones deshonestas, la concupiscencia desordenada y la avaricia, que viene a ser una idolatría [Col. 3:5].
> ... en suma: desnudaos del hombre viejo con sus acciones [Col. 3:9]
> y vestíos del nuevo, de aquel que por el conocimiento de la fe se renueva según la imagen del que lo creó [Col. 3:10]
> para con el cual no hay distinción de gentil y judío, de circunciso y no circunciso, de bárbaro y escita, de esclavo y libre; sino que Cristo es todo, y está en todos. [Col. 3:11].

Osuna chooses this basis on which to defend the convert (see Chapter IX). The "new man," to Paul and to Osuna, is a reality that could easily be mistaken for a figure of rhetoric. Both are alike, too, in seeing the necessity for conscious moral reform following the rebirth in baptism. I do not, however, see in Paul the suggestion of renewed baptism through contemplation, although his statement of the *symbolic* value of rituals seems to leave the way open for this.

Osuna's dialectic treats at length the idea of rebirth attached to the word *alumbrado*. Does this mean that he was a member of the sect? It seems possible that the term could have been loosely applied to people who felt themselves to be reborn or enlightened in spiritual exercises. Osuna's own works, with their wide distribution, must have done their share to help define the term in the public mind. A belief in the literal efficacy of this rebirth led Osuna to defend the convert; perhaps it had a similar influence on others. Probably we shall never know whether Osuna was sent to France and Belgium in 1532 to avoid confrontation with authorities persecuting either *alumbrados* or *conversos*. If such were the case, he returned undaunted, and his ringing defense of new Christians, along with criticism of the ecclesiastical hierarchy, was printed in the Fifth Alphabet (1542). Before assigning him to the martyr's category, however, it must be noted that his forthright statements on these subjects go uncensored.

As might be expected, the Pauline idea of regeneration through baptism was too attractive to be let alone during the course of centuries. Thorndike reports that in the early Christian period a Gnostic sect, the Elchasaites, practiced re-baptism for the remission of sins. At such times they invoked seven "witnesses:" heaven, water, holy spirits, angels of prayer, oil, salt, earth (*Magic*, I, 373). Is it only a coincidence that these items apears in Osuna's treatise 4, which deals with a renewed spiritual baptism? Gnostic notions were sometimes preserved in alchemical treatises, of which we have seen plentiful suggestions in Osuna. Research into such materials would be in perfect consonance with Osuna's interest in the world of nature; the science that, to him, brought the most joy.

Figurative Language. In the process of explaining the figures of this treatise, an anagogical level has been constructed by using canons of the figures supplied by Osuna, by Scripture, and by Christian tradition.

The process of contemplation, as Osuna describes it, consists of working with the canons of the figures, comparing them to each other and making deductions. Each figures of the treatise can be seen to have canons relating it to other figures, and to the Divine. Each one seems to be a nucleus, with relationships extending everywhere. As a result, all the creatures are sanctified; "y cada cosa criada / en Dios vuelta en otra cosa." [9]

As far as I have discovered, this treatise is Osuna's most ambitious attempt at stimulating the reader to try his own wings in contemplation. Should the reader fail to do so, he may miss one of Osuna's most significant statements on the nature and purpose of *recogimiento*.

---

[9] From *Estímulo del divino amor*, a poem attributed by some to Luis de León (cited by Menéndez y Pelayo, in *La mística española*, ed. by P. Sainz Rodríguez (Madrid, 1956), 191.

Since the anagogical level is carried almost entirely by unexpressed canons of the figures, the treatise appears to be a radical attempt to give a coherent exposition almost entirely by figures used as though they, themselves, were words in a sentence. We are forced to read the meaning of the figures to "translate" the treatise.

The reader is first notified that he should seek unexpressed meaning by the character of the introduction to the theme, which is a *praeteritio*. Here, the symbol of the two-headed man summarizes the duality that prevails in the treatise, and especially in the introduction, where Osuna delivers a curse that may be read as a blessing.

The reader is confirmed in his feeling that a hidden meaning should be found when he notices the prevalence of the concept *arca*, and begins to suspect that the ship is Noah's Ark.

The presence of important and well-known figures such as the Ark, the tree of life, and the fountain in Paradise immediately suggest unexplored anagogical possibilities. So does the somewhat awkward insertion of the anecdote about St. Vincent. It recalls Osuna's statement that anomalies in Scripture are a signal that a spiritual meaning should be sought. Other suspicious factors, to the careful reader, are the lack of a logically satisfying development in the literal level of Treatise IV, culminated by the change of subject in Treatise V, and the strange assertion that it occupies the third position.

In Treatise IV, Osuna has used a technique of concealment and suggestion. He hid the Ark of Noah, for example, and used it for an unexpected secondary characteristic, the bilge. Similarly, in the two figures from IV Kings 4, he explicated the less obvious one.

Since any figure, taken with all its canons, tends to suggest numerous others, Osuna could have planned the treatise first in terms of some major figures suitable to his theme. Apparently, he worked from the general concept to its particular exemplars, in the case of *arca*. Other figures were probably inserted with a view to completing or emphasizing certain canons of the major ones. The final list of figures looks like an effort of this sort. The St. Vincent story seems to be an effort to bring the Word into relation with the sword, in order to force the reader to postulate a canon that both may have in common. Sequential order is meaningful, as in the case of the hawk, which is followed by the figure of the Good Shepherd (God Himself ultimately "recollects" the contemplative soul) (*3 Abc.*, 328). Apparent incongruities are included in order to force the reader to attempt their resolution.

Withal, Osuna does develop in the figures an adequate *dilatatio* of his theme: "Guarda tu corazón con toda guarda, porque dél procede la vida." "Toda guarda" refers not only to the rejection of sin (contrition), but also the stilling of the senses in *recogimiento*. The heart, container of the Divinity within, is the baptismal font in which the reformed Christian is born.

As for the position of Treatise IV as the middle term of a triad, I believe that it forms, with Treatise III, a *narratio* in the series of *exordium, narratio, conclusio*. At the same time, it seems to belong to the series of the three hierarchical acts (in which it represents illumination especially), and beginning, middle, and end — middle in the sense also of "means," for *recogimiento* is the means by which the soul finds God. This meeting is a real experience of a spiritual Presence (*3 Abc.*, 569). The treatise therefore corresponds, as it should, to the Beatitude: "Blessed are the pure in heart (*los recogidos*); for they shall see God" (Mt. 5:8).

If the animal, vegetable and mineral "creatures" of this treatise are steps in the *scala coeli*, it can be seen that their progression is from particular to general, and from one level of abstract interpretation to another, with a consequent revelation of analogical patterns. (We saw this technique applied to a simple Scriptural text concerning the eagle.) Through correspondences, several figures fuse into a simpler reality, or into an abstract. The progression is from multiplicity toward unity.

The use of such highly figured language seems to be an attempt to create in the reader a certain psychological effect; one that may have some resemblance itself to the flight of the contemplative's spirit. The reader's attention is intensely engaged in an attempt to perceive and retain the figures, with their numerous canons, which are presented in rapid succession. As analogies among the canons begin to appear, a pattern is seen, and the resulting simplification has the force of a "marvel," or "revelation." It is an experience like that of sudden insight or total recall, which seems to come with no effort, after great effort. This psychological release of tension may perhaps resemble, in a lesser degree, the flight of the contemplative soul into the Empyrean, after the intense concentration of meditation.

If this be so, Osuna was guided in his formulation of this treatise by preoccupations that might be called aesthetic, as well as doctrinary. He has attempted to create in the reader the sensation of his own experience. Because of the nature of this experience, the "language" that he chose was that of poetry. He used figures that brought with them a multiplicity of connotations. The mutual analogies and contrasts among these give rise to further meanings, that seem to appear from nowhere, because they are not to be seen on the printed page. I think we can consider these to be the invisible "spirit of the letter."

The reader can participate in this experience only if the figures carry, for him, approximately the same connotations that they had for Osuna. This must have been anticipated by Osuna himself; the first two Alphabets and the earlier treatises of the Third contain much of the information needed to read this treatise effectively. Also necessary is a retentive memory, to which Osuna attaches great importance.

The aesthetic effect of the treatise depends on the reader's previous indoctrination, and on his undivided concentration. For the success of this type of poetic, both reader and writer must collaborate, and they must have a ground of common knowledge.

In describing his own style, Osuna chose to compare his technique to polyphony. The metaphor seems peculiarly suitable to this treatise, where different items, abstract or concrete, present similar patterns of function. The principal themes are expressed in canonical forms or patterns, all of which harmonize into a fairly simple design that might be called the final "chord." And just as the occurrence of certain musical notes suggests or demands in the hearer the occurrence of others, the unseen tenors of Osuna's figures suggest or demand resolution and fulfillment of the pattern.

Because of the multiplicity of factors that Osuna has succeeded in uniting into Treatise IV, he may well call it an "espiga," as he does (by implication). Just as the figures hide the meaning of the treatise, the treatise is hidden in the rhetorical organization. The successive veils must be penetrated before the Divinity is discovered. So that the sanctuary may not pass unnoticed, however, Osuna leaves a clue for the unwary one (el que "no verá cuando viniere el bien") who has arrived at the fifth treatise without tasting the substantial fruits of the fourth.

Chapter IX

THE ALPHABETS: STYLE AND CONTENT

The plain style. It is the figured style of Osuna that requires explanation, but it is by no means the only aspect of the Alphabets. Osuna puts moral statements into very clear language, so that there is little chance of misinterpretation.[1] In such passages, Osuna takes to task not only the individual, but also his contemporary society. Although he may sometimes conceal his anagogical doctrines, his stand on moral and social issues is unequivocal. For example, he criticizes the policies of the feudal lords in expanding the *latifundios,* asks for intervention in business monopolies, and decries artificial manipulation of the currency exchange, wars, and corruption in the Church (*5 Abc.*, fols. 209-12). He speaks of the unfair business practices of the merchants in Antwerp, and says that the kings, "que también toman a logro," must share the blame, as well as the wise men, who ought to show people what is right (*5 Abc.*, fol. 199). He notes than most of the world is in the hands of tyrants and half of the church in the hands of the greedy (*5 Abc.*, fol. 28).

He defends the convert, saying that all baptized people are of Christ's lineage; the corporal progenitor of all mankind is the earth. The Jew and the Gentile are figured in the twins that fought while still within the mother's womb (Gen. 25.c), "y el más ruin [el pueblo gentílico] se lleua la ventaja." To hold against a Christian his carnal origin is a mortal sin (*1 Abc.*, fols.

---

[1] In this, it appears that he models himself on Scripture, following the observation of St. Augustine that moral guidance is always plainly stated there. Mazzeo, *Studies,* 5.

121-22). Father de Ros points out that in 1525 the Franciscans ruled that no one would be received into the Order "que fuesse de linaje maculado dentro del cuarto grado" (citation from Pedro de Salazar, *Crónica y historia de la provincia de Castilla*, Madrid, 1612) (de Ros, *Maître*, 28, n. 1). Osuna's views of the matter, published in 1528, are obviously in conflict with the policy of his Order, but he states them as clearly and forcefully as they can be put.

As for the Jews themselves, Osuna declares that Christ's martyrdom was caused by the sins of the world, present ones as well as past. The Jews have now paid for their sin, and should not be blamed. Rather, one should reprehend his own sins before castigating those of others (*6 Abc.*, fol. 84).

Osuna's idea of equality extends to a genuinely democratic principle. He cites Seneca to the effect that "riches and tyranny" inspired some people to call themselves better than others — that is, nobles. To be a "noble" (an aristocrat) says Osuna, is not a trait of the person himself but is rather the opinion of others. All trees produce good and bad fruit; "tal es el padre tal es el hijo" only applies to the divine Persons. Seneca said that one person was more noble than another only if he were more intelligent. Christian nobility lies in the friendship of God and the grace of the Holy Spirit (*1 Abc.*, fols. 122-23). The book in which this appears is dedicated to Juan Tellez Girón, conde de Ureña, apparently Osuna's long-time protector, and certainly an aristocrat by birth.

In the Second Alphabet, Osuna says that if kings all come from one lineage, some will be bad. Election of a ruler is preferable, although not perfect (*2 Abc.*, fol. 153).

The emperor Carlos is richer than his grandfather Fernando, but he will sweat from his ears before he wins victories as great as those of the Catholic king (*6 Abc.*, fol. 47).

On the subject of religion, Osuna says that "la libertad cristiana" can exist in prison, and offers the case of St. Paul as an example (*5 Abc.*, fol. 66). In the folio immediately preceding, he has deplored the calumnies of the rich against those whom they wish to despoil. The suggestion is, perhaps, significant, and may refer to some denunciations heard by Inquisition tribunals.

Heretics should not be threatened with fire, but should be cured by wholesome doctrine, sweet admonitions, and prayer (*6 Abc.*, fol. 22). (Earlier in his life, however, Osuna had justified the burning of heretics in one of his Latin works (de Ros, Maître, 162 and n. 3). This is one instance of a development in Osuna's ideas, which appear to become more liberal and independent with age.)

As far as external penance and similar observances are concerned, unless there is participation of the spirit as well as the body you could do them until Judgment day, and they would be worth nothing (*2 Abc.*, fol. 101).

Free will is too precious to be lightly cast away; Christ never took a vow to obey every fool, as those do who enter religious orders, and are subject to the whims of thirty Pilates. Therefore, is you are inclined to religion, it might be just as well to practice it at home (*5 Abc.*, fols. 136-37).

Osuna's plain-spoken opinions and robust morality are among the most attractive features of the Alphabets, and he demonstrates a surprising boldness considering the historical moment. When he "conceals" his doctrine, it seems likely that his purpose is to stimulate meditation, since he does not lack the courage to speak on most questions. Moreover, the ecclesiastic censor probably read Osuna's figured style more easily than we do today. In religious doctrine, he was, apparently, orthodox enough.

Osuna's passages in plain style range from the purely didactic through the affective and the entertaining. He varies the tone frequently to avoid monotony. The reader is addressed personally ("tú, hermano") and Osuna is now impressive, now stern, satiric, confidential, consoling, cheerful, witty — whatever seems most suitable to the material and to the moment.

In the passages of relatively plain language, Osuna's imagistic mode of thought shows itself in apt similes. His sensitivity to language levels can be seen in his use of the strong contrast between the ideal and the material. An extreme example is the set of Goliardic responses to the Ten Commandments. In the First, God asks of a penniless soldier if he loves Him above all other things. The soldier answers: "What things?..." (*5 Abc.*, fols. 187-88). Plays on words and concepts are frequent.

Osuna's simple style is sufficiently flexible to serve as an instrument for any purpose. In contrast to the work of his contemporaries Alejo de Vanegas and Alonso de Madrid, Osuna's has an extraordinary intimacy, grace and color. There is considerable variation of tone in Osuna's works, and his technical mastery, of course, increases with time.

All the Alphabets contain a mixture of clear and figured styles. Instructional material, including moral doctrine, is given in plain language; figures carry "spiritual wisdom." Both are necessary; he who will not carry on corporal works as well as spiritual ones is "un sancto de pie quebrado" (*3 Abc.*, 525).

The figured style. To convey anagogical material (which may include postulates of natural science) Osuna often uses the figured style that invites meditation. He introduces these passages as a method of developing his themes. On such occasions, one passage may lend itself to several different readings, since figures have many canons, and may be interpreted on several levels. Osuna himself says that contemplation is an individual matter. However, the writer of spiritual exercises, when he determines the literal words, establishes the canonical form that other levels must follow. By explicit insertions of allegorical, tropological, or anagogical material, he suggests how these levels should be developed. By precept and example, Osuna trains the reader in the processes of induction and deduction necessary to find the spirit hidden in the letter.

Osuna scatters through the Alphabets enough data on most of his figures to permit several levels to be extracted from almost any figured passage. This is not to say that the possibilities are exhausted by the material that Osuna gives. He omits some of the traditional connotations of many figures. The character of the genre is determined by its aim to incite meditation and contemplation, the course of which will vary with the reader's experience.

In his numerous explications of themes, Osuna gives the reader information about figures and words; this must be remembered and applied. It is for this reason that Osuna emphasizes memorization of his material. Only when the memory can supply most of the canons of a figure will the reader see a coherent pattern emerge from the mass of details. Such patterns appear to conform to philosophical ideas, some of which are expressed by Osuna in plain words. However, the hasty reader may easily fail to recognize any relation between the abstract statement and its appearance in figurative guise. This is one of the factors that has contributed to the impression of disorder in the Alphabets, and to some misunderstandings of their content.

Osuna has maintained the importance of mental images in meditation. His figures are most communicative when they are visualized. The imagination shows clearly why a sailing ship may symbolize the Cross, or a snake may represent the liquid mercury. Not only do the shared canons become evident, but also, the reader experiences the sensation of discovery.

Figures as a memory aid. Another motive for exposition through figures is the factor of memory retention. For the contemplative, as Osuna says, this is a serious problem. Those who contemplate by either the positive way (the creatures) or the negative one (*recogimiento*) complain of forgetting, which hinders their progress (*6 Abc.*, fol. 69). Osuna's explanation of memory shows a materialistic theory of the mental image. He says that in memory we keep "masks" of the people that we see. We cannot remember our own faces as well as those of others, because the real person makes a stronger "impression" (used in the literal sense of *imprimere*, I believe) than "delicate image" from the mirror.

Forgetting is a spiritual death; it snatches things from our senses and memory as death takes them from the present life (*6 Abc.*, fols. 69-70). Osuna's suggestions for improving memory include avoiding moist foods and eating dry ones, such as raisins and almonds. (Vapors from wet foods rise to the head and disturb the memory.) But more important, he says, is to concentrate on the item you want to remember to the exclusion of everything else. Still more important is to love the thing very much. Another aid is to converse with people who have the same interest (*6 Abc.*, fol. 71).

Although Osuna does not include it explicitly in this list, the process of "softening" the heart to receive the mental image (mentioned in Chapter III as an emotive factor) probably is also a memory aid. In such a materialistic view of mental imagery, the importance of receptivity would be recognized. Also, the emotional attitude created by dramatic visualization would tend to cause retention of the image; this is probably one of the ideas included in that of "loving" the thing that is to be remembered.

Osuna's use of the figure as a vehicle for exposition is probably motivated by recognition of its emotive effect, its staying power in the memory,[2] and its aesthetic appeal (*flectere, docere, delectare*). The medieval preaching theorists (cited in Chapter V) remarked that figures have the advantage of being retained in the memory. This attribute was noted by Cicero.[3] Obviously, a long tradition recognized the figure as a mode of knowledge easily retained in the memory. Pedro de Ravena (whom Osuna mentions at least three times in the Fifth Alphabet: fols. 14, 142, 202) is the author of a treatise on the art of memory (*L'Artificiosa memoria seu Fenix*, Venice, 1491).[4] This treatise is based on Ciceronian theory (Rossi, "Immagini," 166). Osuna's comments on memory, however, are almost exclusively common-sense. I do not recognize in his work any reference to artificial aids other than alphabetical ones, unless the geometric figures that he introduces (rather sparingly) may suggest some influence of the Ars Magna of Ramón Llull (Vasoli, "Bruno," 255). Osuna considers emotion — love — the most important factor in memory. Retention of information or of mental images is important because it is a requisite for spiritual exercises.

The science and art of contemplation. The practice of meditation and contemplation, as Osuna shows it, would lead to an extremely comprehensive body of data about the universe. In effect, his works are a reconciliation of the books of the "creatures" (science and human experience) with Christian doctrine. The canons that govern one govern all. These canons are not always expressed in abstract terms. Often; they appear in the form of created beings with the attributes that can be predicated to them. These figures stand as surrogates for human and divine characteristics. The significance that they come to have does not always correspond to the connotation of their names in ordinary

---

[2] Alphabetical order is also one of his memory aids; he suggests, for example, putting the kinds of love into order by ABC and learning them for the purpose of meditation (*3 Abc.*, 508).

[3] *De Oratore*, II, 86-88; cited by Paolo Rossi, "La costruzione delle immagini nei trattati di memoria artificiale del rinascimento," in *Umanesimo e simbolismo* (Padova, 1958), 168-69 and n. 1.

[4] Cesare Vasoli, "Umanesimo e simbologia nei primi scritti lulliani e mnemotecnici del Bruno," in *Umanesimo e Simbolismo*, 251.

language. The only way in which Osuna's universe may be perceived is by visualizing the terms with their new connotations.

Osuna's mixture of didactic and affective preoccupations prevent the Alphabets from being classified either as entirely philosophic, or completely aesthetic. They can probably best be termed simply meditations. Their inherent structure might be called vertical; that is, they proceed from the physical world "upward" to the metaphysical and "down" into the psychological, or from the particular to successive abstractions. The aim of knowledge and emotion is to see the right course of action and to awaken sufficient motivation to pursue it.

Osuna's expositions are often structured on the basis of the figure, with its predications and its relation to other figures. These give the Alphabets an intrinsic organization that is different from their extrinsic one, which is founded on abstract generalities and their subdivisions. The universe that Osuna depicts for contemplation consists of figures that are interrelated as are the things of the natural world; that is, they do not necessarily lend themselves to a linear logical treatment, nor to ordinary linguistic categories. Rather, any figure becomes a center from which radiate canons, the significance of which can be displayed and which show their relation to other creatures or to spiritual realitites. While several figures may have canons in common, as did the serpent and the two-headed man, they also have an unalterable individuality that is always present to the consciousness. Although some of the canons coalesce, because of their relationships, into abstracts, the creature itself still remains. I believe that this aesthetic effect is sought because it portrays the view of reality represented by the Logos. Every created thing is a part of one Totality, and in some way represents it; some relation should therefore be perceivable in the individual parts. This relationship will be "spiritual," or abstract. On the other hand, each creature is a distinct idea in the mind of the Logos, so that its individuality is not only warranted but sanctified.[5]

The reader will probably have noticed that when the highly figured Treatise IV was explicated, the procedures of meditation

---

[5] Compare the theory of names in Fray Luis de Leon, in which the diversity of creation is united in the mind, *Obras completas castellanas* (Madrid: Biblioteca de Autores Cristianos, 1951), 396-97.

described by Osuna were employed. Memory supplied the "predicables" of the figures, reason discursively produced their canons. As abstract patterns formed, similarities were seen, and these abstracts were manipulated in the process of contemplation. When the whole picture is conceived, intuitive knowledge has been reached — the simultaneous, "pictorial" representation of a complex but unified structure. The mind in this phase seems full to bursting with a multiplicity of forms, which can be retained only by virtue of their relationship to the dominant canon. Intense concentration is required, and this concentration brings the excitement of discovery, and the "illumination" of seeing harmony in discord. Therefore, Osuna conducts us through a spiritual exercise to discover for ourselves what he has elsewhere said in plain words. But "la gloria de Dios está en esconder la palabra: y la gloria de los reyes en la investigar." (Pr. 25a, *Convite*, fol. 75).

Osuna's interest in natural philosophy impelled him to give it an unusual importance. Osuna attributes to the creatures the qualities predicated of them by science and by Scripture. He seems to have a wide acquaintance with science, and accommodation of the sources is facilitated by his metaphorical interpretation of the Bible, and his ability to refer to its Greek, Hebrew and Chaldean versions. To traditional sources, Osuna has added some observations that may be from his own experiences.[6] With this material, he has composed meditations that show an extensive and well-developed view of the universal order. The Alphabets are encyclopaedic in scope, and their philosophy is fundamentally consistent throughout. Although other commentators have remarked that there is little relation among the six books, each one really develops parts of this philosophy, which unifies the group.

---

[6] Osuna emphasizes the value of experience in learning. For example, he says that Christ came to the earth seeking "sabiduria por experiencia," although he already had infused wisdom. Experience is esteemed by the wise; it composes all the arts and creates all books. In man, the science of books is of little value without experience. Christ's wounds are signs of experience, like the doctor's cap (6 *Abc.*, fols. 74-77). Possibly Osuna respects experiential learning the more because it is the only way to the superior cognition of *recogimiento* (3 *Abc.*, 569). His attitude may also reflect the tradition of Roger Bacon and of the Ockhamists, who promoted learning through observation of reality rather than exclusively by authority.

The "alphabet" that they teach consists of figures and concepts that are new categories for the discrimination of realities. Osuna's statement that spiritual exercises are the words of God is a working premise; the letters are creatures and concepts; for the words of God are the Creation. In our discussion of Treatise IV of the Third Alphabet, I believe we saw some of these "letters" and we may have constructed a syllable or word.

To compose such complex works as the Alphabets, the writer must have had a phenomenal memory and a considerable library. Although concordances, collections of "sentencias" and other handbooks for preachers would have been helpful, they could hardly have supplied the basic philosophical principles, nor the ability to manipulate consistently the quantity of material, that the Alphabets display. This would have to arise from a clear understanding of principles that could govern the arrangement of many details. Osuna must be considered, I believe, one of the outstanding intellects of his day.

Osuna's ideas and style in historical perspective. This serious and ambitious plan to unite science and revelation has antecedents in the work of another Franciscan, Ramón Llull, and in that of Ramón Sabunde. Similar tendencies appear among the Italians of the fifteenth century, among them Ficino, with his efforts to reconcile neoplatonism and Christianity, Pedro de Ravena with his memory aids to enable the scholar to encompass more data, and Nicolas de Cusa. Later, the same encyclopaedic tendency appears in Camillo (Rossi, "Immagini," 173-174) and Vico ("Immagini," 162), for example, both of whom also espoused the use of figures for the embodiment of concepts to be understood and retained.

When Osuna makes his appearance on the scene, the encyclopaedic tradition, like the preaching tradition, was already so well developed that it is difficult to speak with assurance of his sources. He shares with Llull many opinions on contemplation, but they could easily have sprung from common origins. Like Sabunde,[7] he sees nature and Scripture as parallel manifestations of the

---

[7] Tomás y Joaquín Carreras y Artau, *Historia de la filosofía española* (Madrid, 1943), II, 140.

Divine. However, the number of common sources is too great to permit influences to be easily traced. For the same reason, it is difficult to determine Osuna's impact on his successors.

Father de Ros has, however, discovered substantial textual borrowings in Fray Luis de Granada, San Pedro de Alcántara, Martin de Lilio and Juan de los Angeles. In respect to Santa Teresa, de Ros modifies somewhat the findings of Etchegoyen, but still finds correspondences. There are also coincidences of doctrine and lexicon in San Juan de la Cruz (de Ros, *Maître*, 617-639). In addition, borrowings from Osuna can be seen in Bernardino de Laredo (*Subida del monte Sion*) and in Bartolomé de los Mártires (*Compendium spiritualis doctrinae*). [8]

The writer most notable for his debt to Osuna is a more famous Franciscan, Antonio de Guevara. The latter borrows freely from Osuna, especially from the First, Third, and Fourth Alphabets. These citations Guevara attributes to St. Ambrose, St. Jerome, Origen, Hugo of St. Victor, and other saints and sages! Father de Ros demonstrates textual borrowings so lightly retouched that one has to conclude that Guevara knew perfectly well the real source of his quotations. [9] When the bookseller Juan de Espinosa dedicated Osuna's posthumous Fifth Alphabet to Guevara, it was a moment of inspired irony, whether purposeful or not. Father de Ros, in fairness to Guevara, also shows some possible influences of Guevara on Osuna in the Fifth Alphabet itself (*Guevara*, 387, n. 65).

Guevara's false attributions indicate that he counted on a substantial degree of ignorance in his courtly public. In this he was not mistaken, since his reputation has overshadowed that of Osuna for four centuries. Could he have been one of those who glossed Osuna's words in a way the latter did not approve (*1 Abc.*, fol. 5)? Certainly, in this case, the world has rewarded the more worldly — and less talented — writer.

It remains for research to pursue the matter of Osuna's influence on non-religious genres. This will be difficult, because of

---

[8] Fidèle de Ros, "Influencia de Francisco de Osuna en Laredo y los Mártires" (*Archivo Ibero-Americano*, julio-sept. 1943, no. 11), 378-90.

[9] Fidèle de Ros, "Guevara, auteur ascétique" (*Archivo Ibero-Americano*, abril-sept. 1946, núms. 22-23), esp. 380-97.

the many sources used by Osuna himself. (Of *his* citations, the ones I have checked have been genuine.) In *El criticón*, for example, there occur many ideas expressed by Osuna, including that of the creatures as revelation of the Creator. However, this concept is so widespread that it would be profitless to try to trace its trajectory.

Osuna's technique of using figures is one aspect that tends to distinguish him among vernacular writers, and to identify his place in the development of literary styles. He represents a distinct advance in flexibility and aesthetic quality within the style of preaching rhetoric. Also, he clearly delineates the figure, both as a philosophical concept and as an instrument of rhetoric. Because of this and because of the wide distribution and imitation of his work, he must be accorded an important place in the history of the "poetic of correspondences" — a popular development of the meditation of the creatures. Another typical feature of Osuna's style is his humor based on changes of "level" — anagogical, literal, and the like. Another notable practitioner of this type of wit is Cervantes.

Osuna's exposition through figures, although it is based on the methods of medieval preachers, may have been reinforced by the symbolism of the Cabbala, publicized by Pico (with whom Osuna shares certain ideas about the mutability of man); or by the new vogue for hieroglyphs. (The Horapollo treatise appeared in Venice in 1505.)[10] The hieroglyph is a "creature" that represents a concept, or a set of concepts; its adaptability to the traditional idea of the figure is obvious. One might be tempted to consider this system responsible for Osuna's attitude toward the alphabet, were it not for the fact that Sabunde (who died in 1432) had also seen a correspondence between the creatures and the words of God (Carreras y Artau, *Filosofía española*, 140), as had Origen, Philo and Tertullian.

A similar force that may have tended to emphasize the use of figures by Osuna is the developing interest, during his time, in emblems, seals, and "impresas." All of these could be classified as visual representations of concepts (although the emblem has its

---

[10] Pierre Mesnard, "Symbolisme et humanisme," in *Umanesimo e simbolismo*, 125.

own history). "Empresa" is a term often used by Osuna in the sense of an impression made by a seal. As he uses it, it stands for the mental image, perhaps the Aquinian "species intelligibilis impressa."

Again, it would be difficult to calculate the influence of hieroglyphs, of the Cabbala, or of the *impresas*, because it is not easy to separate their contributions from those of Osuna's older sources; an ancient exegetical and iconographic tradition, reinforced by a study of philosophy and a natural science that probably included allegorical treatises on alchemy. The Friars Minor of the Observance (Osuna's branch of the Franciscans) were specifically ordered to give up their "occult" books in 1591 (Thorndike, *Magic*, VI, 150-51).

Noticeable in Osuna's work is his alternation between the creature itself and the abstract concept, without the intervention of the personifications, such as pagan gods or allegorical personages that were so often used by the Italian neoplatonists. This may result from a desire to simplify, or from the dictates of taste or censorship, or, perhaps, from the fact that Osuna's theory of contemplation leads away from "corporal" images. The result is a sort of "magic realism" in which the reader sees through the material object into its abstract meanings. The visible world becomes an Alexandrian landscape, the residence of exiles from the world of the spirit.

The poetic of correspondences. The art of tracing correspondences in canons of figures was a necessity in the traditional method of Biblical exegesis, and also in the exposition of themes through multiple connotations of words and figures. In the seventeenth century, Gracián will define the *concepto* as "un acto del entendimiento, que exprime la correspondencia que se halla entre los objetos.... Esta correspondencia es genérica a todos los conceptos, y abraza todo el artificio del ingenio, que aunque éste sea tal vez por contraposición y desonancia, aquello mismo es artificiosa conexión de los objetos." [11]

The first *décima* given by Gracián as an example is the following:

---

[11] Baltasar Gracián, *Agudeza y arte de ingenio, en que se explican todos los modos y diferencias de conceptos* (Madrid, 1929), 7-8.

> Caminante: esta urna breve
> guarda un Sol resuelto en hielo,
> convertido en tierra un Cielo,
> una estrella en polvo leve.
> No el cetro en los reyes mueve
> a ser de su ser ajenos;
> de llanto los ojos llenos
> llega, y tu reina verás;
> viva, no pudo ser más,
> muerta, no pudo ser menos. [12]

Here, the contrasts of "great-small," "heat-cold," etc., fill an abstract pattern that might be called "reversal of the nature of a being" "being alien to one's being." (The term *concepto* seems to be applied by Gracián to the abstract pattern that is filled.) The procedure consists of "meditating" on the figures utilized, and abstracting from them canons that bear out the abstract concept; or reversing the order and seeking figures with canons that will bear out a preconceived abstract. In this meditation, memory must retain the figure, while dialectical processes, by noting "distinctions in essence or accidents" (Gracián, *Agudeza*, 8), elicit the appropriate canons, and logic defines the abstract "whole" that they form. This is the procedure of meditation, as Osuna describes and demonstrates it. The aesthetic effect of successful conceptistic poetry also is to create the intuitional "picture" in the mind, as in contemplation.

Just as Osuna attempted to create in the reader the sensation of sudden insight, "marvel" or revelation, so does the metaphysical poet. Mazzeo [13] has collected the comments of several Italian critics on *acutezza*; Pellegrini probably shows most clearly the revelation of unity in multiplicity that was the objective of the "artful" revelation of the correspondances between objects. Considering the role played by Aristotle's ten categories in the determination of these correspondences, it is not strange that the Italian critics Tesauro and Pallavicino claim Aristotle as their intellectual father.

---

[12] Attributed by Gracián to Antonio de León; *Agudeza*, 4.

[13] Joseph A. Mazzeo, "A Seventeenth-Century Theory of Metaphysical Poetry" (*Romanic Review*, XLII, 1951), 245-55.

Gracián distinguishes two types of "agudeza": perspicacity and artifice. The first seizes upon difficult and recondite truths; the latter seeks "subtle beauty." The first is "art and science, in its acts and habits," the second "has no fixed home." It is the latter that is the subject of Gracián's treatise (*Agudeza*, 9).

Since both perspicacity and artifice are sub-classes of *agudeza*, it is natural that their methods are similar; in fact, they employ similar dialectics. Gracián recognizes *agudeza* in religious works; he cites many in the course of his book.

Osuna's works, because they purvey recondite truths, should be classed with "perspicacity," although they show at times a surprising degree of "artifice." The intellectual processes of meditation, in the Alphabets, are designed to reveal the sacred universe, and the reader is forced to develop "perspicacity" in order to discover hidden wisdom. Osuna comprehends and explicates both philosophy and rhetoric. To him, both are sanctified, for both reality and language are manifestations of God. His philosophical preoccupations make him, moreover, a more profound explicator of the bases of *agudeza* than is Gracián.

Unlike the poets in Gracián's collection, Osuna uses his dialectic in the service of science as well as for the production of effects. His method, which is based on rather rigorous inductions and deductions, has within itself a validity unrelated to the nature of the data it manipulates. Osuna's information includes picturesque elements from tradition, as well as more rigorous ideas from Aristotle and St. Augustine, among others; and, probably, some observation.

Whatever the character of the data (which may be fantastic, like the attributes of the phoenix or carbuncle), the result of the dialectical treatment is an impression of phychological validity useful to rhetoric, though sometimes irrelevant to science.

Osuna does not give his data and methods with the primary intention of compiling an encyclopaedia of knowledge. He uses this material in meditations designed to teach a technique of contemplation, to incite emotions, and to produce a changed pattern of action in the reader. In his search for psychological effects, he has produced at least one instance of a substantial discourse composed principally in figures, all of which contribute to the formation of one complex concept. As the figures tend to free themselves from the context of prosaic exposition, and to communicate in their own right, Osuna's meditations approach the character of poetry. As such, the Alphabets form an intermediary step between the figures as a device of perspicacity and their use as an element of poetry. In the poems of San Juan de la Cruz, they appear without the matrix of exposition (which is consigned to another work), and the poetic tendency reigns supreme. In the conceptistic poets of Gracian's collection, the dialectical processes of meditation appear as an element of poetic technique. Their logical character is made clearly evident by Gracián's own analysis of them. However, they no longer pretend to reveal sacred truths; rather, they are used for their aesthetic effect. In fact, the same techniques may be applied to grossly mundane material.

In the development of conceptistic style and symbolism, scholars have mentioned the influence of classical rhetoric and the mnemotechnic devices that sprang from it; of Petrarchian figures, emblems and hieroglyphs. To this list should be added, I believe, the medieval art of preaching. Battlori has pointed out the influence of Aristotelian rhetoric, with its "topics" or figures, through which, he says, the *ratio studiorum* of the Jesuits developed an aesthetic of free invention, stimulated by emblems and *impresas*.[14] Osuna's Alphabets show already a richness of symbolism that is hardly to be exceeded by any later writer.[15] Many of his figures or topics are derived from traditional Christian sources whose influence has been little studied, but which may well be as important as those mentioned by Battlori. In addition, the question of possible Hebrew sources is yet to be resolved.

In the manipulation of figures, both Osuna and the poets whom Gracián selects use techniques developed by the medieval preachers, and based, ultimately, on the exegetical tradition.

From these resources there may arise a poetic that exploits the figures in their own right, as is seen in San Juan de la Cruz. Or the dialectical technique may dominate, resulting in manifestations of *conceptismo*.

Although Osuna's figures and phrases occur from time to time in the works of later writers, the problem of common sources

---

[14] Miguel Battlori, *Gracián y el barroco* (Rome, 1958), 104-10.
[15] Osuna and St. Ignatius Loyola (1491-1556) are practically contemporaries.

makes tracing of direct influence difficult, unless there is a substantial body of discourse in common. Nevertheless, in the Spiritual Alphabets may be found stylistic trends that illuminate relatively unexplored aspects of the literature of the sixteenth and seventeenth centuries. Among these are the figures and the techniques of their use, which can be seen in the context of a philosophy and rhetoric that governed them. Osuna developed resources of expression adequate to his own heterogeneous material, and to his affective and logical ends. These resources are united, in the Alphabets, with instructions to the reader on how the material should be pursued. It is seldom that any writer offers, by precept and example, so much information about his theory and practice. To the student of a period of complex literature, such insights may be helpful, as they may also have been helpful to Osuna's contemporaries and immediate successors. For them, Osuna performed the important service of placing spiritual exercises (mental prayer) in the context of a systematic philosophy, an active life and a rhetorical method. The popularity of his works attests to his importance as a conveyor to the public of the wealth of Biblical information, philosophy and tradition accumulated in the cloister. In Osuna's case, learning is illuminated by a vital enthusiasm for knowledge from whatever source — ancient or modern, christian or non-christian, experimental or deductive — and by a genuine love for that Janus-headed monster, man.

To convey this varied material, he developed a vernacular prose rich in resources of style, and a vocabulary ranging from the most learned to the most colloquial. His works certainly anticipate, and may even have radically influenced, the magnificent flowering of vernacular literature that took place in the Golden Age.

INDEX

Aaron, 72
abstract. *See* concrete-abstract, figure, Biblical exegesis.
acutezza, agudeza, 165-66
aeon, 143-44.
   See also snake.
air, 114-15, 117-18, 122. *See* elements.
afecto, efecto, 43-46
Alcántara, San Pedro de, 162
Allegory. *See* levels of Biblical interpretation, Biblical exegesis, figure.
Alphabets, 12-18, 23-26, 57-58, 97, 144, 151, 158
   scriptural alphabets, 57-58
altar, 111, 132
alumbrados, 19-21, 147-48, addenda.
alumbrar, 71-74, 111.
   See also light, birth.
Ambrose, St., 53, 93
amplification, 22-23, 90, 96-98
   See also Biblical exegesis.
analogies, 24, 27, 38, 88, 165
   See also words, figure.
Ángeles, Juan de los, 162
angels, 42, 61, 81, 148
   cherub, 109, 133
   seraph, 142
animals, 59, 73
   tail of, 76
   wild beasts, 88-89
   passions, 121
   animals of sacrifice, 132
   goat's blood, 128
   See also creatures *and* individual species.
Apocalypse, woman of, 139, 142
Aquinas, St. Thomas, 50, 66, 85, 137
Arcana, 4˙, 97, 133

Aristotle, 86-87, 114, 116, 139
   on friendship, 43
   reasoning, 66
   ten categories, 86-87, 165
Ark, 133-37, 139, 149
   of the Covenant, 109, 132-33
   of Noah, 129, 134-37, 149
ascension, 62
asceticism, 46
Assisi, St. Francis of. *See* Francis of Assisi, St.
Augustine, St., 32, 44, 48, 84, 114, 118, 138, 153
Ávila, St. Teresa of. *See* Teresa of Ávila, Sta.

baptism, 75-76, 129-31, 135, 145-48, 150
   baptismal water, 35, 123, 128
Bataillon, Marcel, 19-22
Beatitudes, 106, 150
Béjar, duchess of, 17
Bernard, St., 36, 56
Biblical exegesis, 23, 27, 80, 82-94, 164
   some sources, 93
   See also amplification, analogies, levels, figure.
bilge, 110, 113
bird, 54, 63, 145
   turtledove, 54
   dove, 128, 133, 145
   See also eagle, hawk.
body, human, 44, 49-50
   sensuality and reason, 45-46
   body and soul, 53-54, 102, 104, 114, 116, 120-23
   heart and blood, 107-19, 124, 128,

134, 136, 141, 145
Boehmer, Eduard, 18
bomba, 110, 116, 134
Bonaventure, St., 41
branch, 132
bread, 41, 101-2, 131
bush, 107, 127-28, 137, 143

Cabbala, 163-64
Canaan, 61
canons, canonicity, 66, 77-78, 151, 159, 164-65
  counterpoint, 38, 63
Canticle of Solomon, 55
Cárcel de amor, 50
castle, 108, 129
cedar, 62
Celestina, 50
Cervantes, Miguel de, 29, 163
chariot of Elijah, 55, 113
charity. *See* love.
Chrysologus, 28
Cicero, 158
ciencia, 57
circle, 38, 107, 119
  See also wheel.
city of God, 43, 137
cloud, 105
concebir, 72-73, 76-77, 138, 141-42, 145, 164
  concept, 91, 96, 134, 161
  See also intellect, generation and birth.
conceptismo, 29, 164-65
concrete-abstract, 40-41, 52, 77-78, 87-88
  See also body, soul, etymologies, language
conocer, 72-73, 78, 105
contrition, 75-76, 78, 146
convertir, 37
converts, attitude toward, 20, 147-48, 153-54
correspondences. *See* canons.
counterpoint. *See* canons.
creation. *See* universe.
  re-creation, 143
creatures, 26, 41, 80, 84, 148-50, 159, 163
  See also animals, elements, universe.
Cruz, San Juan de la, 24, 162, 167

cube, 140
custom, habit, 46, 75-76

deer, 63
democratic principles, 154
de Ros, Fidèle, 13, 15, 18, 22, 162
diamond, 107, 128, 137
Dionysius the Pseudo-aeropagite, 33-34, 146
docta ignorantia, 46
door, 95, 137
  to heart, 113, 128
  See also wound.

eagle, 60-63, 73, 74, 144
earth, 44, 106, 129, 139, 140, 148
  See also elements.
ecstasy, 19, 34, 55, 63, 133
Elchasaites, 148
elements, 34-35, 121-23
  love as, 34
  as components of body, 44-45, 120, 133
  See also air, earth, fire, water.
Elijah, 55, 113
Elisha, 138, 140
emanations, theory of, 32
emblems, 163, 167
emotions, 34, 91
  place in spiritual exercises, 94-96
Empedocles, 118
Erisistratus, 118-19
escalera, *See* ladder.
espiga, 96, 112
Espinosa, Juan de, 16
Espinosa, Pedro, 142
essence and attribute, 31-32, 165
  of God, 31-32, 59
Etchegoyen, Gaston, 18, 27
etymologies, 40-41, 80, 88
Eucharist, 60, 121, 131-32, 146
Eve, 45
eye, 73
  eyes of mind, 72
  eye of God, 82
  See also sight.

farsa, 95-96
Ficino, Marsilio, 103, 118, 120
figure, 26, 28, 58-60, 62-63, 67-68, 77-78, 85-91, 99-100, 112, 148-51, 156-68

See also canons, creature, painting, word.
fire, 44, 48, 56, 77, 109, 111, 121-23, 125-27, 145
  See also elements.
Form, reform, 52, 62, 123-24, 131, 139, 141, 146-47
  and function, 87
  See also concebir, figure, matter, soul.
fortune, book of, 80
fountain, 130, 137
  of love, 48
  of grace, paradise, 109, 129-31
Francis of Assisi, St., 46

Galen, 115, 117
garden, 130-31, 137
  See also paradise, terrestrial.
generation and birth, 34, 70-74, 138-41, 145
  See also intellect, concebir, alumbrar.
gold, 34-35, 46
goodness, object of will, 31, 38
  proportional to entity and to substance, 31-32
grace, 20, 44, 50-53, 105, 109
  See also love.
Gracián, Baltasar, 164-66
Gracioso Convite, 13, 15, 18
Granada, Fray Luis de, 162
Groult, Pierre, 22
Guevara, Antonio de, 16, 162

Harvey, William, 115
hawk, 107, 125-28, 150
head, 23, 107, 120, 127, 137, 143-44, 149
heat, 34, 35
  See also love, sun, steam.
Hebrew sources, 20, 57-58, 80, 118
hermeneutics, sacred, 84-86, 87-93
  See also figure, etymologies, Biblical exegesis.
Hernández, Francesca, 13-14, 18
heron, 126
hieroglyphs, 163
honey, 42, 53
host, 131-32, 134
  See also Eucharist, bread, wheat.
house, country, 109

of sport, 109
of God, 137
Hugo of St. Victor, 43
Humors, 114, 120

Ibn An-Nafis, 115, addenda
illumination, 56, 160
  See also alumbrar, fire, intellect, sabiduría, sapere.
imagination, 65-66, 95
impresas, 163-64, 167
incarnation, 59-62, 70, 73
intellect, 31, 34-36, 38, 70-75, 77-79, 88, 105, 112-113, 159
intelligence, 61, 64-66
  reason, 65-66
  See also soul.
iron, 37

Jacob, 88-90
Jesús, Crisógono de, 29
Jews, attitude toward, 153-54
John the Evangelist, St., 62-63

knife, 109, 126, 127, 132
  See also sword.

ladder, 80-81, 150
  Jacob's, 80
lance, 83, 108
language, 76-79
  See also alphabets, words, tilde.
law: of love, Chap. 2, positive vs. natural, 31
  tablets of, 102, 109, 133
Lebanon, 62
León, Fray Luis de, 32, 148, 159
letters. See alphabets, words.
levels of Biblical interpretation, 23, 82-83, 89, 97-99, 156, 163
  See also Biblical exegesis.
light, 35, 63, 72-75, 77
  in oxymorons, 77
  See also sun, sight, intellect.
Lilio, Martín de, 162
lion, 59, 75
Llull, Ramón, 158, 161
Logos, 95, 98, 102, 133, 141-44, 159
  See also word, concept, heart.
Longinus, 83
love, Chap. 2, 69, 71-72, 75, 76, 83,

89, 94-95, 98, 104, 111, 114, 119, 120-22, 124-28, 145
Lucifer, 40

manna, 95, 109, 132-33, 140
Mary and Martha, 81
Mary, Virgin, 62, 72, 111, 137-140, 142
matter, 52, Chap. 3, 139
　See also elements, body, concrete-abstract.
memory, 113, 133, 151, 156-58, 160, 165
　memory aid, 97, 158
　See also soul.
mercury, 110, 122-23, 128
　mercurial principle, 144
microcosm, 57
　See also body, soul.
Mirandola, Pico della, 163
mirror, 47, 49, 82, 84
"Missus est," alter sermonum super, 16
"Missus est," expositionis super, 16
moon, 35-36, 142
Moses, 102, 105
motion, laws of, 39-40
mountain, 56, 73, 102, 105

Names, Divine, 32, 159. See also words.
Norte de los estados, 13, 29
numbers, 58, 140
nuptials, 125, 145-46

oil, 110, 138, 148
Origen, 49, 55, 163
original sin, 45
Ortiz, Francisco, 13, 18
Osuna, Dukes of, 14, 154

painting, 38, 58-59, 75, 96
　See also figure.
parable. See word.
paradise, terrestrial, 109, 129-31, 133-34, 137
Pars meridionalis, 16
Pars occidentalis, 16
passions, 55
　functions of will, 55, 113-14
　See also wheel, will, soul.
Peers, Allison, 13

Persiles y Sigismunda, 29
Pfandl, Ludwig, 22
Philo, 80, 138, 163
pig, 59, 75
present tense, invariable, 71
pump, 49, 110, 115, 118

Quijote, don, 29, 96

rainbow, 134, 136-37
Ravena, Pedro de, 158, 161
reason. See intellect.
redemption, 60, 70
reform. See form.
religious freedom, 154-55
resurrection, 61, 72, 73, 130-31
Richard of St. Victor, 64, 133
rock, 140
rod, 109, 125, 132, 133, 137, 140
Rodríguez Marín, Francisco, 13

sabiduría, 48, 57, 130, 137-39, 166
　See also intellect, sight, conocer, concebir, alumbrar.
Sabunde, Ramón, 161-62, 163
St. Victor, Hugo of. See Hugo of St. Victor.
St. Victor, Richard of. See Richard of St. Victor.
Sainz Rodríguez, Pedro, 18
salamander, 34
salt, 88, 106-107, 128-29, 148
Sanctuarium biblicum, 16
Santa Teresa, Nazario de, 22
sapere, 35, 75
Sarraute, Michel-Ange, 13, 16, 18, 22
Saturn, 144
Scotus, Duns, 33, 119
Scriptures, 80, 82
　Evangile, 60
　Old Law figure of New, 70
　See also Biblical exegesis.
seals, 59, 75-76, 96, 164
　See also figure, contrition.
Selke de Sánchez, Ángela, 20
sepulchre, 130-31
Servet, Miguel, 115, 119, addenda.
sheep, 88-89
　lamb, 95
　ram, 132
　lost, 108, 131

INDEX

See also shepherd.
shepherd, 88-89
   as lover, 51
   with lost sheep, 108, 131
   Good, 150
ship, 134-35, 137
   See also ark of Noah, bilge.
sight, 60-61, 63-65, 73, 77-78
   negative after-image, 77
   See also light, painting.
smelting, 37, 52, 121
snake, 59, 75, 123-24, 126, 129, 131, 142-44, 146
soul, Chap. 2, 87, 106-24, 127-29, 132-34, 136, 139, 141-43
   contained in heart, 54
   God's memory, 49, 54
soul, mother of, 48
space relations, 77
steam, sublimation, vapor, 109, 121-25
   boiling over, 55, 111, 125
sublimation. See steam.
substance-attribute, 32
sun, 34-36, 49, 73-74
Sunamitess, 140
sword, 101-102, 108-109, 123, 125, 126, 127, 132, 144

tarasca, 144
Teresa of Avila, Sta., 13, 162
Tertullian, 80, 163
tilde, 76
tree, 109, 112, 114, 130-31, 137, 144-45
   See also branch.
triad, 102-104, 106, 150
triangle, 107, 112
Trilogium evangelicum, 16

universe, 41, 57, 58, 63-64, 75
   as image of God, 57, 58, 60, 69,
80, 82, 92, 99-100
   as depicted by Osuna, 159, 166
   See also creatures.

vacuum, 42, 49
vapor. See air, steam.
vessels, of the widow (IV Kings 4), 110, 137-38
   of gold, 111, 137
Vincent, St. 108-109, 149
virtues: faith, hope, charity, 54

water, 44, 48, 111, 121-25, 129-32, 148
   sweet and bitter, 48
   See also elements.
Weynsen, Mathias, 18, 93
wheat, 101
   yerba, espiga, grano, 106
wheel; of Elijah's chariot, 55, 113
   of Ezechiel's vision, 109, 121
   of the passions, 113, 120-21
   of time, 143-44
   See also circle.
widow of IV Kings 4, 110, 137-39
will, 31, 40, 47-56, 88, 105, 108-109, 112-113, 121, 126, 129, 133
   See also love, soul.
winds, 113, 121, 144
wine, 41, 53, 131-32
wings, 80
words (and letters), 57-59, 78-80, 101-102, 123, 126-27, 145, 160-61, 164, 166
   and parables, 66-67
   classifying by function, 78-79
   letters of the *Alphabets*, 97-100
wound, 83, 95, 145

zodiac, 125
Zurbarán, Francisco de, 142

ADDENDA

Since this book was written I have encountered several texts in which the reader may be interested. One is a study of Osuna's rhetoric by Judith A. Marquis: "Las imágenes en los *Abecedarios Espirituales* de Francisco de Osuna" (unpublished dissertation, Ohio State University, 1970). Another is a more general study of rhetoric by Charles Faulhaber, *Latin Rhetorical Theory in Thirteenth and Fourteenth Century Castile* (Berkeley, 1972). In *Corrientes espirituales en la España del siglo XVI* (Trabajos del II Congreso de Espiritualidad) mention is made of the influence of the Nordic mystics in Osuna (J. Sanchis Alventosa, "Los escritores nórdicos y los espirituales españoles," 527-542). In the same collection is a study by Luis Sala Balust: "En torno al grupo de alumbrados de Llerena" (509-523), that includes a considerable bibliography on illuminism. An article by Antonio Márquez entitled "Origen y caracterización del iluminismo" (RO, XXI, 1968, 320-33), may also be of interest. I should not neglect to mention that *Corrientes espirituales* begins with a very useful bibliography; it comprises Part I.

In reference to the history of theories on the circulation of the blood, Dr. José Barón Fernández has included in his study of Servet (*Miguel Servet: su vida y su obra*, Madrid, 1970), a synopsis of the theories of Ibn An-Nafis, with the information that several copies of his manuscripts are still to be found in Spain although no copy of the study on circulation is yet known there. The possibility of its transmission to Italy is discussed. An Andalucian of Osuna's time could easily have had access to Arabic materials at home; also, he made a voyage to North Africa. The Franciscans, because they accepted scientific data from non-

Christian sources, could be expected to be the more ready to take cognizance of such a theory. Publication of it could have been restrained by its theological implications. Servet included his treatise on circulation in a work on theology, says Dr. Barón Fernández. It is worth noting that he begins with a statement similar to Osuna's idea: "El espíritu divino está en la sangre y el espíritu divino es él mismo la sangre o el espíritu sanguíneo" (*Servet*, 167). It is a vapor generated of air, fire and water; air is supplied in the lungs. Servet bases his theory on Old Testament statements: Genesis 9, Leviticus 7, Deuteronomy 12 (*Servet*, 123-131). Clearly, it is essential to Servet's theory that air ("spiritus") travel in the blood, and not through separate vessels. Osuna seems to believe this. Although this implies that air enters the blood, Osuna does not say how, as Servet does.

Servet apparently knew Hebrew and was entrusted with the preparation of a new edition of the Bible (*Servet*, 129-131). If Old Testament ideas on the blood and the spirit formed the basis of circulation theory, they could have inspired Jews, Mohammedans, and Christians alike. In Spain, the three religions had lived in constant contact. An idea known to one could easily and comprehensibly have been transmitted to the others. Besides the opportunity for mutual influence, the three religions used common sources: Greek science and the Old Testament. A study of Osuna's Latin works might clarify his position in respect to circulation theory.

NORTH CAROLINA STUDIES IN THE ROMANCE LANGUAGES AND LITERATURES

I.S.B.N. Prefix 0-88438

Recent Titles

STUDIES IN HONOR OF MARIO A. PEI, edited by John Fisher and Paul A. Gaeng. 1971. (No. 114). -914-6.

DON MANUEL CAÑETE, CRONISTA LITERARIO DEL ROMANTICISMO Y DEL POS-ROMANTICISMO EN ESPAÑA, por Donald Allen Randolph. 1972. (No. 115). -915-4.

THE TEACHINGS OF SAINT LOUIS. A CRITICAL TEXT, by David O'Connell. 1972. (No. 116). -916-2.

HIGHER, HIDDEN ORDER: DESIGN AND MEANING IN THE ODES OF MALHERBE, by David Lee Rubin. 1972. (No. 117). -917-0.

JEAN DE LE MOTE "LE PARFAIT DU PAON," édition critique par Richard J. Carey. 1972. (No. 118). -918-9.

CAMUS' HELLENIC SOURCES, by Paul Archambault. 1972. (No. 119). -919-7.

FROM VULGAR LATIN TO OLD PROVENÇAL, by Frede Jensen. 1972. (No. 120). -920-0.

GOLDEN AGE DRAMA IN SPAIN: GENERAL CONSIDERATION AND UNUSUAL FEATURES, by Sturgis E. Leavitt. 1972. (No. 121). -921-9.

THE LEGEND OF THE "SIETE INFANTES DE LARA" (*Refundición toledana de la crónica de 1344* versión), study and edition by Thomas A. Lathrop. 1972. (No. 122). -922-7.

STRUCTURE AND IDEOLOGY IN BOIARDO'S "ORLANDO INNAMORATO," by Andrea di Tommaso. 1972. (No. 123). -923-5.

STUDIES IN HONOR OF ALFRED G. ENGSTROM, edited by Robert T. Cargo and Emanuel J. Mickel, Jr. 1972. (No. 124). -924-3.

A CRITICAL EDITION WITH INTRODUCTION AND NOTES OF GIL VICENTE'S "FLORESTA DE ENGANOS," by Constantine Christopher Stathatos. 1972. (No. 125). -925-1.

LI ROMANS DE WITASSE LE MOINE. *Roman du treizième siècle.* Édité d'après le manuscrit, fonds français 1553, de la Bibliothèque Nationale, Paris, par Denis Joseph Conlon. 1972. (No. 126). -926-X.

EL CRONISTA PEDRO DE ESCAVIAS. *Una vida del Siglo XV,* por Juan Bautista Avalle-Arce. 1972. (No. 127). -927-8.

AN EDITION OF THE FIRST ITALIAN TRANSLATION OF THE "CELESTINA," by Kathleen V. Kish. 1973. (No. 128). -928-6.

MOLIÈRE MOCKED. THREE CONTEMPORARY HOSTILE COMEDIES: *Zélinde, Le portrait du peintre, Élomire Hypocondre,* by Frederick Wright Vogler. 1973. (No. 129). -929-4.

C.-A. SAINTE-BEUVE. *Chateaubriand et son groupe littéraire sous l'empire.* Index alphabétique et analytique établi par Lorin A. Uffenbeck. 1973. (No. 130). -930-8.

THE ORIGINS OF THE BAROQUE CONCEPT OF "PEREGRINATIO," by Juergen Hahn. 1973. (No. 131). -931-6.

THE "AUTO SACRAMENTAL" AND THE PARABLE IN SPANISH GOLDEN AGE LITERATURE, by Donald Thaddeus Dietz. 1973. (No. 132). -932-4.

When ordering cite *ISBN Prefix* plus last four digits given with each title.

Send orders to:
    International Scholarly Book Service, Inc.
    P.O. Box 4347
    Portland, Oregon 97208
    U.S.A.

www.ingramcontent.com/pod-product-compliance
Lightning Source LLC
Chambersburg PA
CBHW020416230426
43663CB00007BA/1189